Essential
Venice

Above: *view from the Campanile*

PASSPORT BOOKS
NTC/Contemporary Publishing Group

This edition first published in 2000 by
Passport Books, a division of NTC/
Contemporary Publishing Group, Inc.,
4255 West Touhy Avenue, Lincolnwood
(Chicago), Illinois 60712–1975 U.S.A.

Above: *gondoliers
are identified by their
distinctive boater hats*

Front cover: *wooden
chalets in mountain
village; astronomical
clock, Bern; woman in
traditional costume*
Back cover: *dairy cow*

The contents of this publication are believed correct at the
time of printing. Nevertheless, the publishers cannot accept
responsibility for errors or omissions, nor for changes in
details given. We are always grateful to readers who let us
know of any errors or omissions
they come across, and future printings will be updated
accordingly.

Published by Passport Books in conjunction with
The Automobile Association of Great Britain.

Written by Teresa Fisher

Library of Congress Catalog Card Number: on file
ISBN 0-658-01105-7

Colour separation: Chroma Graphics (Overseas) Pte Ltd,
Singapore

Printed and bound in Italy by Printer Trento srl

Contents

Teresa Fisher's Venice

Getting Your Bearings

Venice is divided into sixths (*sestieri*): San Marco, San Polo, Santa Croce, Dorsoduro, Cannaregio and Castello. San Marco contains the main city sights, while Cannaregio is one of the least touristic, though containing some of the city's most beautiful canals. Two natural waterways define the city – the Grand Canal, which coils snake-like, dividing the city into two, and the Giudecca shipping channel to the south.

Above: *glass shop displaying the sort of exquisite wares you can expect to find in Venice*
Right: *the Bridge of Sighs was made famous in Byron's* Childe Harold

For centuries Venetians and visitor alike have been spellbound by Venice, the most breath-takingly beautiful and extraordinary city, equal parts stone and water; a floating city laid out on 200 tiny islands with 'the sea for its floor, the sky for its roof, and the flow of water for walls' (Boncompagno da Signa, 1240).

Even though it has been painted, photographed, written about and filmed more than any other city in the world, nothing can prepare you for the first powerful impact of Venice – it may be the gondola down the Grand Canal when the city is enveloped in the mists of winter, or when the setting of the summer sun bathes the city in the magical pinks, blues and golds so beloved by artists such as Titian, Veronese and Canaletto, but it is guaranteed that your first impressions will be memorable.

Few cities can offer such artistic richness as Venice. For many cnturies, as the gateway to the Orient and under the medieval leadership of the Doges, the city ruled as a world capital and a

mighty sea power, and its immense wealth was celebrated in art and architecture throughout the city. Today, with the glories of this heritage evident at every turn, you could easily mistake Venice for a painting come alive, a stage set full of real people, an open-air museum.

Venice is no museum, but rather a living and fragile city; a miracle of survival despite its decaying foundations, the encroaching water and rising silt. Although, contrary to popular belief, it is officially 'no longer sinking', its ominously tilting bell-towers stand as testimony to the city's ephemerality, as concerns mount about increasing levels of pollution from nearby industrial towns, which are irreparably corroding the city's ancient stonework. This is to say nothing of the rapidly dwindling population, as modern houses, jobs, plans for a metro and other attempts to preserve Venice for the Venetians clash with those aimed at preserving the city for posterity.

When we leave Venice, our memories will not only be of its beauty and art treasures, but also of city life – pasta alfresco in a peaceful sun-splashed piazza; the gentle swaying of gondolas tied to gaily striped mooring poles; the sights and scents of local markets; buildings reflected in the still water of the canals, shop windows brimming with Carnival masks and dazzling glass displays; or even St Mark's Square flooded on a high tide. For this is the magic of Venice, which entices devoted visitors back year after year to *La Serenissima* – the 'most serene', and captivating, city in the world.

Santa Maria della Salute, at the entrance to the Grand Canal

Gondolas
Gondolas were first recorded in 1904. In the 18th century there were 14,000 in use. Today there are around 400, all made to the same design: 10.87m in length, with a maximum width of 1.42m. The hull is asymmetrical – 24cm wider on the left than on the right – to assist with steerage. Each gondola is made out of 280 parts, made from eight different woods – fir, cherry, walnut, larch, mahogany, oak, lime and elm – and, according to 16th-century law, are all painted with seven layers of black lacquer.

Floating market in San Barnaba

Venice's Features

Mooring poles add colour to the murky canal water

The City
- Height above sea-level: 31 inches (80cm)
- Height of 1966 floods: 6 feet (2m)
- Highest point: Campanile at 300 feet (99m)
- Size of city (from east to west): 8 miles (5km)
- Size of city (from north to south): 3 miles (2km)
- Size eqivalent to: Central Park, New York
- Number of districts (*sestieri*): 6
- Number of canals: 170
- Number of bridges (estimated): 400
- Number of alleys (estimated): 3,000
- Number of churches (estimated): 200
- Rate of sinking (annual): 0 inches
- Buildings on Grand Canal with damaged foundations: 60 per cent
- Visitors per year (estimated): 12 million

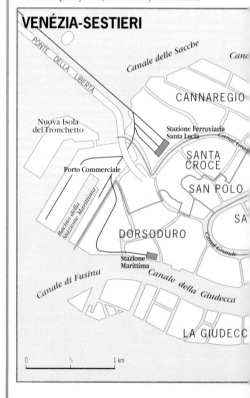

VENÉZIA-SESTIERI

PONTE DELLA LIBERTA

Canale delle Sacche

Cana

CANNAREGIO

Nuova Isola del Tronchetto

Stazione Ferroviaria Santa Lucía

Canal Grand

SANTA CROCE

Porto Commerciale

SAN POLO

Bacino della Stazione Marittima

SA

DORSODURO

Canal Grande

Stazione Marittima

Canale di Fusina

Canale della Giudecca

LA GIUDECC

0   ½   1 km

Population
• Population in heyday of Venetian Republic (estimated): 200,000
• Population in 1950 (estimated): 140,000
• Population in 1998 (estimated): 68,000
• People leaving Venice annually due to high prices, lack of jobs and housing: 1,500 (est)

Economic Factors
• Cost of living: 1 per cent higher than Milan, 3 per cent higher than Rome
• Percentage of workforce involved in tourism: over 50 per cent
• Number of souvenir shope (estimated): 450
• Number of plumbers (estimated): 13

The Lagoon
• Length: 30 miles (56km)
• Width: 5–9 miles (8–14km)
• Surface area: 550sq km
• Number of islands: 34

Palazzo Mocenigo used to belong to one of Venice's finest families

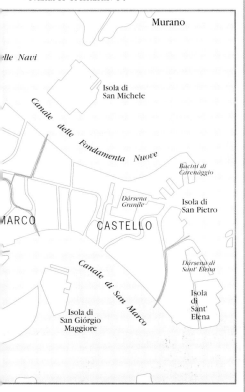

Essence of Venice

Carnival masks are often intricate works of craftsmanship

Gondolas pointing towards the island of San Georgio Maggiore

Venice is a city which charms and captivates, the historic flagship of a mighty fleet of islands in the lagoon, the most photogenic city in the world.

To discover its true character you should first see the main sights – the Grand Canal, St Mark's Square, the Doges' Palace. But then take time to explore the picture-postcard backwaters with their hidden squares and tiny churches.

There's a secret side to Venice too, only accessible by water. Once afloat, you enter a different world, seeing the city as it was designed to be seen, through snatched glimpses into ancient houses, secluded gardens, and boatyards with gondolas waiting for repair. This is where the real essence of Venice lies.

THE **10** ESSENTIALS

If you only have a short time to visit Venice, and would like to take home unforgettable impressions, here are the essentials:

• **Take a boat** (and plenty of film!) along the Grand Canal by day, to marvel at its majestic water-lapped *palazzi* and gaily painted mooring poles, or by night to catch glimpses of the grand illuminated interiors.

• **Visit the Rialto markets** (➤ 44) at the crack of dawn before the crowds arrive.

• **A mid-morning coffee** in Europe's finest square, atmospheric St Mark's (➤ 16), will both delight and bankrupt you.

• **Stroll along the southern shore** of the Dorsoduro, with its boathouses, bars and cafés (➤ 18). Go at dusk, when Venetians take their *passeggiata*, or promenade.

• **Indulge yourself** in the romance of a gondola ride at sunset and capture the true magic of Venice.

• **Take the lift** up to the top of the Campanile (➤ 42) or San Giorgio Maggiore (➤ 34) for breathtaking views.

• **Watch the world go by** from the terrace of a Venetian classic, Harry's Bar, whilst sipping on a Bellini cocktail (➤ 74).

• **Get lost in the labyrinthine alleys** and backwaters of the city, or visit the outlying islands (➤ 53) for a taste of Venetian life off the main tourist drag.

• **See Venice by night.** The canals have a magical beauty and many of the main monuments are floodlit.

• **End your day Venetian-style** with an ice-cream or a *digestif* in one of the city's countless café-ringed squares.

Above: *red is the gondoliers' colour*
Below: *relaxing in a waterfront café*

The Shaping of Venice

A 14th-century manuscript showing Marco Polo leaving Venice

8th century BC
The Veneti and Euganei tribes are the first to settle in the lagoon area.

3rd century BC
Veneto conquered by the Romans.

402
Alaric the Goth sacks Altinium; its inhabitants flee to the lagoon, guided by a vision of the Virgin.

421
Venice traditionally founded on 25 April, St Mark's Day.

453
Attila the Hun sacks Aquileia, prompting another exodus of refugees to the lagoon.

466
Lagoon's settlements elect 'maritime tribunes' to govern.

697
Maritime tribunes appoint the first Doge (leader) of Venice – Paoluccio Anafesto.

814
First Venetian coins minted; work begins on Doges' Palace.

828
Venetian merchants steal the relics of St Mark from Alexandria.

829
Work commences on the Basilica di San Marco.

1000
'The Marriage to the Sea' ceremony (➤ 98) is inaugurated to celebrate Doge Pietro Orseolo II's defeat of Dalmatian pirates in the Adriatic.

1094
Basilica di San Marco is consecrated.

1095
Venice provides ships for the First Crusade.

1204
Venice sacks Constantinople in the Fourth Crusade and acquires much of the former Byzantine Empire.

1271
Marco Polo leaves Venice for the Far East.

1348
The Black Death kills half the population.

1380
The Battle of Chioggia: Venice defeats the Genoese, thereby proving its unrivalled maritime supremacy in both Adriatic and Mediterranean.

1406
Venice defeats Padua and Verona to lay the foundations of a mainland empire.

1450
Venice's power reaches its height.

1453
Constantinople falls to the Turks, ending Venice's trading privileges.

1514
Fire destroys the original timber Rialto bridge.

1571
Venice loses Cyprus to the Turks but Battle of Lepanto is decisive victory for the western fleet, including Venice.

1669
Venice loses Crete to the Turks.

1718
Surrender of Morea to the Turks marks the end of the Venetian maritime empire.

1752
Completion of sea walls protecting the lagoon entrances.

1797
Napoleon invades Italy; the last doge abdicates

Don John of Austria defeats the Turkish fleet in the Battle of Lepanto

and the Venetian Republic comes to an end.

1814
Following Napoleon's defeat Venice and the Veneto are ceded to Austria.

1846
Rail causeway links Venice to the mainland for the first time.

1848
First Italian War of Independence. Venice revolts against Austrian rule.

1866
Venice joins a united Italy.

1881
Venice becomes the second largest port in Italy after Genoa.

1895
First Biennale art exhibition.

1902
The Campanile in Piazza San Marco collapses (rebuilt by 1912).

1932
First Venice Film Festival.

1960
Venice airport opens.

1966
Floods cause devastation. UNESCO launches its 'Save Venice' appeal.

1973
Laws passed to reduce pollution, subsidence and flooding.

1978
Patriarch Luciani of Venice elected Pope John Paul I, but dies 33 days later.

1983
Venice officially stops sinking (after extraction of underground water is prohibited).

1988
Work begins on the lagoon's flood barrier.

1995
Centenary of Biennale Exhibition.

1996
La Fenice opera house is destroyed by fire.

NAVALIS · PII · V · AVSPICYS · DE · TVRCIS · AD · NAVPACTVM · PARTA · VICTORIA

Venice's Famous

An Honorary Venetian
In 1949 Peggy Guggenheim, the famous American copper heiress and modern art collector, purchased the most eccentric *palazzo* on the Grand Canal to house her outstanding art collection and her retinue of poodles. An honorary citizen of the city, she stayed in Venice until her death in 1979, and is buried (together with her dogs) in the *palazzo* gardens.

Marco Polo
Marco Polo was born in Venice in 1254. At the age of 18 he set out with his merchant father on a four-year overland voyage to the court of Mongol prince Kublai Khan. Here he worked as a diplomat for 17 years, travelling through China and the Far East, returning home in 1295. Three years later he was captured by the Genoese at the Battle of Curzola. In prison, with the help of his cellmate, he put his adventures down on paper, and the *Description of the World* was for long Europe's most accurate account of the Far East. Once freed, he returned to Venice and died in 1324.

Antonio Vivaldi
Vivaldi was born in Venice in 1678. Although ordained as a priest, he devoted his life to music, working as a violin teacher and choirmaster at the orphanage attached to the church of La Pietà (▶ 31). He wrote many of his finest pieces for La Pietà, including 454 concertos and the well-known *Four Seasons*, and the church became famous for its performances. Sadly, music tastes changed and in 1740 Vivaldi left Venice to seek work in Vienna. He died a year later and was buried in a pauper's grave.

Above: *Vivaldi*
Below: *Casanova*

Giacomo Girolamo Casanova de Seingalt
Italy's greatest lover, Casanova, was born in Venice in 1725. Though destined for the priesthood, his dissolute behaviour led to his expulsion from the seminary. Exiled from Venice for five years, he soon discovered his real vocation in the bedrooms of Europe, and was in due course forced to flee Paris, Vienna, Dresden and Prague as a result of various scandals. Returning to Venice in 1755, he was imprisoned at the Doges' Palace for sorcery, but made a daring escape one year later, returning to a debauched lifestyle in the capital cities of Europe. After a period in Spain he returned to Venice as a spy for the Inquisition, but was soon forced to flee once more. He spent his remaining years as a librarian for a Bohemian count. He died in 1798.

J. CASANOVA
DE SEINGALT.

WHAT TO SEE IN VENICE (VENÉZIA)

City Layout

Most of Venice may be a maze of canals and alleys but there are particular places where people walk or gather, usually *campi* (squares) or *fondamente* (waterside promenades). The city is divided into six *sestieri*: to the north and east of the Grand Canal, San Marco is in the centre, Castello to the east and Cannaregio to the west; to the south and west, Dorsoduro lies across the Grand Canal from San Marco with San Polo, then Santa Croce to the north (► map, 6–7). The aquatic highway by which most of the *sestieri* are reached is the main street of the city and that is, of course, the **Grand Canal.**

The Grand Canal

Following the course of an original creek through the muddy islands of the lagoon, the serpentine canal sweeps in two great curves from what is now the Santa Lucia railway station to the Basin of San Marco. It varies in width from 130 to 230 feet (40 to 70m), has a maximum depth of 18 feet (5.5m) and is crossed by three bridges – the Scalzi, the Rialto and the Accademia – and seven *traghetto* (ferry gondola) routes.

Several illustrated guides are devoted solely to the Grand Canal (notably *Canal Grande: Illustrated Tourist Guide* by Lucio Raccanelli; John Kent's *Venice* devotes many pages of illustrations to it) and the better maps will identify the most important buildings.

Travelling eastwards along the Grand Canal, some of the principal buildings between the railway station and the Rialto Bridge are, **on the left-hand side**, the Scalzi, San Geremia and San Marcuola churches and the palaces Ca'Labia (Tiepolo frescoes), Ca' Vendramin-Calergi (the Municipal Casino in winter) and the Ca' d'Oro (museum and art gallery). **On the right-hand side** are the San Simeone Piccolo and San Stae churches, the palaces Fondaco dei Turchi (Natural History Museum), Ca' Pesaro (Galleries of Modern Art and Oriental Art) and Ca' Favretto (Hotel San Cassiano) – and then the fish, fruit and vegetable markets just before the Rialto Bridge.

Between the Rialto and the Accademia bridges are, **on the left-hand side**, the church of San Samuele and the Ca' Mocenigo (where Lord Byron began to write *Don Juan*; not to be confused with the Palazzo Mocenigo which is open to the public) and Ca' Grassi (exhibitions centre); **on the right-hand side**, the palace Ca' Rezzonico (museum of 18th-century arts) – then, at the Accademia Bridge, the Accademia Gallery in the former church and *scuola* of Santa Maria della Carità.

Between the Accademia Bridge and the Basin of San Marco are, **on the left-hand side**, Ca' Barbaro (where many artists and writers stayed and Henry James wrote *The Aspern Papers*), Ca' Grande (Prefecture of Police), Ca'

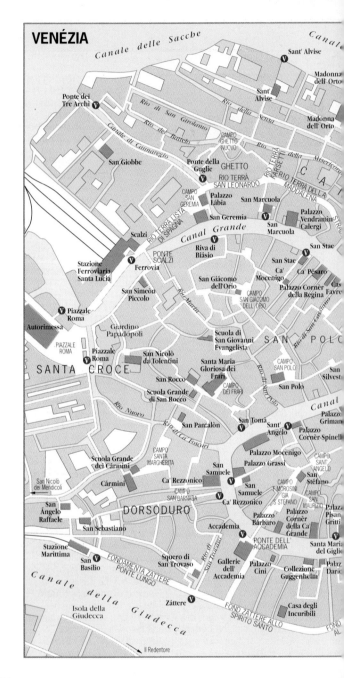

VENÉZIA

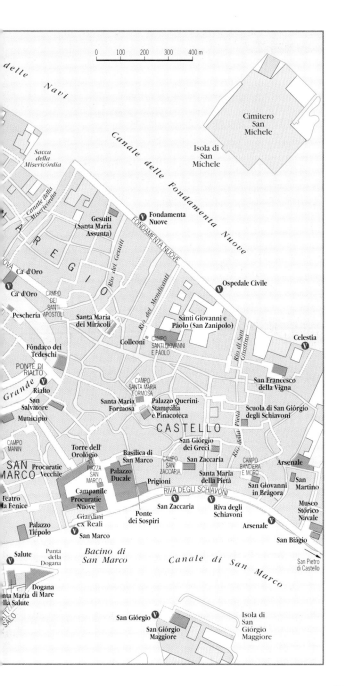

delle Navi

Canale delle Fondamenta Nuove

Cimitero
San
Michele

Isola di
San
Michele

Sacca
della
Misericórdia

Canale della Misericordia

Gesuiti
(Santa Maria
Assunta)

Fondamenta
Nuove

FONDAMENTA NUOVE

CANAREGIO

Ca' d'Oro

Ca' d'Oro

Rio dei Gesuiti

Pescheria

CAMPO
DEI
SANTI
APOSTOLI

Santa Maria
dei Miracoli

Rio dei Mendicanti

Santi Giovanni e
Páolo (San Zanipolo)

Ospedale Civile

Celestia

Fóndaco dei
Tedeschi

Colleoni

CAMPO
SANTI GIOVANNI
E PÁOLO

Rio di San Giustina

PONTE DI
RIALTO

Grande

Rialto

San
Salvatore

Municipio

CAMPO
SANTA MARIA
FORMOSA

Santa Maria
Formosa

San Francesco
della Vigna

Palazzo Querini-
Stampália
e Pinacoteca

Scuola di San Giórgio
degli Schiavoni

CAMPO
MANIN

CASTELLO

SAN
MARCO

Procuratie
Vecchie

Torre dell'
Orológio

Basilica di
San Marco

San Giórgio
dei Greci

Rio della Pietà

Teatro
la Fenice

Campanile
Procuratie
Nuove

PIAZZA
SAN
MARCO

Palazzo
Ducale

Prigioni

CAMPO
SAN
ZACCARIA

San Zaccaria

Santa Maria
della Pietà

CAMPO
BANDIERA
E MORO

Arsenale

San
Martino

Palazzo
Tiépolo

Giardini
ex Reali

San Marco

Ponte
dei Sospiri

RIVA DEGLI SCHIAVONI

San Zaccaria

Riva degli
Schiavoni

San Giovanni
in Brágora

Arsenale

Museo
Stórico
Navale

Salute

Punta
della
Dogana

Bacino di
San Marco

Canale di San Marco

San Biágio

San Pietro
di Castello

nta Maria
la Salute

Dogana
di Mare

San Giórgio

Isola di
San
Giórgio
Maggiore

San Giórgio
Maggiore

0   100   200   300   400 m

Check your watch with the Torre dell' Orologio in Piazza S Marco

Gritti-Pisani (Gritti Palace Hotel), Ca' Tiepolo (Europa e Regina Hotel) – and then the buildings around the Piazza San Marco.

On the right-hand side are the church of Santa Maria della Salute and the palaces of Ca' Venier dei Leoni (the unfinished palace housing the Peggy Guggenheim Collection of Modern Art), Ca' Dario (its façade richly inlaid with multi-coloured marble) and, at the extreme end, the Dogana di Mare (the Customs House), viewable from outside only. The whole length of the Grand Canal is covered by the Nos 1 and 82 *vaporetto* routes.

Piazza San Marco

The Piazza San Marco is the heart of Venice. When Napoleon conquered the Venetian Republic he called it 'the most elegant drawing-room in Europe', and so it still

and the Café Quadri, once patronised by the Austrian occupiers of Venice. On the south side are the former administration building, the **Procuratie Nuove,** with another arcade of shops and the Café Florian, the favourite of Venetian patriots during the Austrian occupation, below. At the western end of the Piazza, the church of San Geminiano was demolished on Napoleon's orders and a new arcade with a ballroom above was built (the entrance of the Correr Museum of Venetian history is now there, ► 51). The two granite columns near the water's edge in the Piazzetta were set up in the 12th century; one is surmounted by a stone Lion of St Mark, the other by the figure of St Theodore, the first patron saint of the city, proudly wielding shield and spear.

Promenades and Squares
The **Riva degli Shiavoni** (The Waterfront of the Slavs) is the principal waterside promenade of Venice, running eastwards from the Doges' Palace to the Ca' di Dio canal, where its name changes; then continuing to the Giardini (public gardens). After the Doges' Palace and the adjoining State Prison comes the Hotel Danieli and a succession of other grand hotels (► 86–8) facing the Basin of San Marco. The wide, paved Riva, broken by a succession of bridges over canals, is cluttered with café tables and souvenir-sellers' stalls at its western end, while its waterside is busy with *vaporetto* piers and the

is. At the eastern end stands the Basilica di San Marco with its Byzantine domes; to one side is its campanile, the Piazzetta outside the Doges' Palace and the Basin of San Marco; to the other the Clock Tower and the Piazzetta dei Leoncini, named after the red marble lions standing there. The north side of the Piazza is bounded by the **Procuratie Vecchie**, the former offices of the Republic's administration, with an arcade of shops below pleasure boats and tugs that moor there.

Leading from the Riva to the north are many alleys and archways running into the maze of the city and to a few squares, notably the Campo San Zaccaria and the Campo Bandera e Moro. Beyond the canal leading to the Arsenale, lie the Giardini, the public gardens, rather dusty and unkempt but with fine tall trees, among which are the pavilions where the Biennale art exhibition is held. This rare open space is where Napoleon demolished the buildings to lay out defensive batteries. There are two churches, the

An original from the artists along Riva degli Schiavoni is an attractive Venetian souvenir

Pietà and the rarely-opened **San Biagio**, near the Naval Museum, along the Riva. The **Fondamenta delle Zattere** is the second most popular waterside promenade, stretching from the docks and the maritime station to the Dogana along the southern shore of the Dorsoduro district and facing across the wide Giudecca Canal to Giudecca island. There are three churches on the Zattere: **Santa Maria della Visitazione**, the **Gesuati** and the **Spirito Santo**. There is also a succession of inexpensive restaurants and two of the smaller hotels (► 74, 89 and 91).

The **Ghetto** – a small district enclosed by canals in the northwest of the city and not far from the railway station – was named after a 14th-century cannon-casting foundry, or *geto* in Venetian. (The name was subsequently given to Jewish enclaves the world over.) Today it remains a centre for that religion. Since Jews were only permitted to live in this small area from 1516 to 1797, they were allowed to build higher houses than elsewhere in the city and so they rise to eight storeys. There are still a number of Jewish families living in the three sections of the Ghetto, as well as synagogues and shops selling Jewish books and souvenirs. In the principal *campo,* a memorial commemorates the Holocaust. *Vaporetto:* Ponte delle Guglie. Throughout the city, *campi,* or squares, are meeting-places and markets for Venetians, often including a parish church, cafés and shops. On the San Marco side of the Grand Canal, they include the **Campo Santi Giovanni e Paolo**, outside the huge church of San Zanipolo (➤ 27), which is dominated by the remarkable equestrian bronze statue of **Bartolomeo Colleoni**, a famous Venetian general of the 15th century. A short walk to the south is the **Campo Santa Maria Formosa** around the church of that name (➤ 37), busy with market stalls and open-air café tables.

On the other side of the Grand Canal, the largest is **Campo San Polo**, where the huge marble well-head is a gathering-place for the young on summer evenings. More lively is the **Campo Santa Margherita**, where stalls sell fruit, vegetables, fish and shoes, and local Venetian life goes on undisturbed by crowds of tourists.

Perhaps the most charmingly Venetian of all the squares is the **Campo San Barnaba** near the Accademia Gallery (*vaporetto*: Ca'Rezzonico). Presided over by the noble façade of the church of San Barnaba (a simple parish church with an air of tranquillity) this bustles with life: shops, two cafés with tables outside and a barge selling vegetables and fruit moored in the canal that connects with the Grand Canal.

Palaces

Few of the scores of Venetian palaces are open to the public

The statue of Carlo Goldini stands watch over the church of San Bartolomeo

and those privately owned are often shuttered and empty, or split into flats. For an idea of their interiors, take a *vaporetto* along the Canal Grande after dark and look up at the lighted windows and you may glimpse paintings in gilded frames, tapestries, frescoes, painted ceilings and chandeliers of Murano glass.

Those palaces that are open to the public are nearly all museums or hotels and are much altered inside. The *palazzi* that are now museums include the **Ca' d'Oro** (Italian art), **Ca' Pesaro** (modern and

19

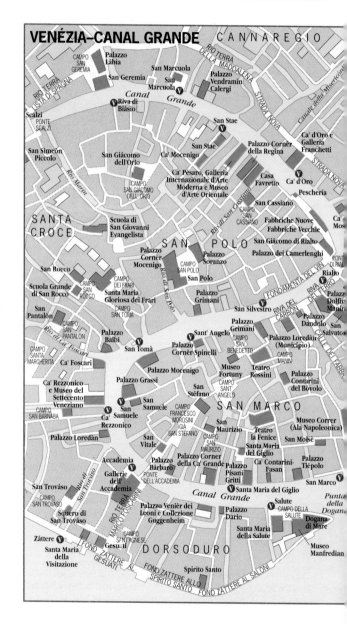

oriental art), **Ca' Rezzonico** (the 18th century), **Mocenigo** (textiles), **Pesaro degli Orfei** (Fortuny), **Querini-Stampalia** (arts) and **Venier dei Leoni** (Guggenheim) – ➤ Museums, 46–53.

There is one palace which every visitor to Venice must see:

♦♦♦
PALAZZO DUCALE (THE DOGES' PALACE)

Piazzetta di San Marco
Venice was governed from the Doges' Palace for a thousand years and it still dominates the city. The pink palace with its white colonnades that we see across the water from the Basin of San Marco, looks much as it did when it replaced an earlier building in the 14th century, except that its pillars seem foreshortened because the level of the surrounding pavement has been raised. Here the elected Doge, or Duke, of Venice held his court and presided over a system of councils, designed to prevent any one self-interested faction seizing power. Once, when this failed, the over-ambitious Doge Marin Falier was convicted of treason and beheaded at the top of the new marble staircase in the palace courtyard and his portrait replaced by a black cloth, which can still be seen. Visitors to the palace can marvel at the succession of richly-decorated council chambers on the second floor, their walls and ceilings painted

21

Arrive early when it's quieter to enjoy the Palazzo Ducale

by the leading Venetian painters, including Tintoretto, whose *Paradise* is one of the largest Old Master paintings in the world. It graces the wall of the Sala del Maggior Consiglio (Great Council Chamber), a vast hall designed to seat 1,700 citizens who had the right to vote in the council. From the Palace itself, the **Ponte dei Sospiri** (Bridge of Sighs) crosses a canal to the prison and the notorious, waterlogged dungeons below water-level known as 'the wells' (*pozzi*). Visitors may join guided tours through the Palace and the prison and also special tours of the 'secret rooms' (in English, French and Italian). This includes the interrogation rooms and torture chamber of the State Inquisitors and the cells under the roof of the prison, called 'the leads', from which Casanova made his dramatic escape in 1756, while serving a five-year sentence on charges involving blasphemy, magic and espionage.

The Doges' Palace is so rich in art and architectural

Other Palaces
The **Palazzo Grassi**, San
Marco 3231, Campo San
Samuele (tel: 041 5231680), on
the Grand Canal, is used for
temporary art exhibitions and
antiques fairs. It is a vast 18th-
century palace with notable
frescoes but was much
modernised in the 1980s for its
present use.
Vaporetto: San Samuele.
The **Palazzo Labia**, on the
Campo San Geremia and the
Fondamenta San Giobbe (not
far from the Santa Lucia
railway station) is now the
headquarters of the Italian
broadcasting service, RAI. It
contains one of the loveliest
rooms in Venice, decorated by
the elder Tiepolo with
gloriously coloured frescoes of
Antony and Cleopatra in 16th-
century dress and dramatic
perspectives.
Open: by appointment 15.00 to
16.00 hours Wednesday,
Thursday and Friday.
Phone to arrange viewing on
the morning of the visit (tel:
041 5242812).
Vaporetto: Ponte delle Guglie.
The **Palazzo Contarini de
Bovolo** can unfortunately only
be seen from the outside. It
does, however, have a
remarkable spiral staircase in
its open courtyard on the Calle
della Vida, close to the Campo
Manin. The Bovolo Staircase
(appropriately, *bovolo* means
snail shell in Venetian dialect)
is a remarkably delicate feat of
architecture and is best seen
by moonlight.
Vaporetto: Rialto or Sant'
Angelo.
Many of the larger hotels were

splendours that a whole
morning or afternoon could be
devoted to it. When Venice is
crowded, it is best to arrive
early to enjoy an unhurried
tour.
Open: daily 08.45 to 17.00
hours, closing earlier in winter.
Tours of the 'secret rooms'
(*itinerari segreti*) leave the
main entrance at stated times,
currently Thursday to Tuesday
three times a day, and must be
booked at least a day in
advance (for more information
telephone 041 5224951).
Vaporetto: San Marco or San
Zaccaria.

23

once palaces and some retain a few of their original internal features. The office of the British Consulate at the Dorsoduro end of the Accademia Bridge is in one of the smaller palaces, Palazzo Querini, and is reached by a marble staircase decorated with *trompe-l'oeil* frescoes.

Churches
Churches are among the greatest splendours of Venice.

The remarkable Bovolo Staircase of the Palazzo Contarini

They may be magnificently simple in design, with white and grey marble expressing baroque beauty or Palladian dignity, or they may be small, like the inside of a jewel-box, whether they date from the Renaissance or the decadent 18th century.

They may be seen as the centrepiece of some great vista across water, or lie hidden in some teeming alley or deserted *campo*.

Church-visiting should be concentrated in the morning, when they are most likely to be

open. Although churches are supposed to be open before noon and from late afternoon until early evening, they are often closed and some seem to be permanently locked. Dedicated church-visitors joke that trying to find the more obscure churches open can be as exciting as stalking rare birds is to ornithologists. Usually, however, a notice by the door will give the times of opening and the times of Sunday services (on Sundays it is best to see the church immediately before or after the service to avoid interruption; otherwise, if a service is in progress, it is courteous to stand silently just inside the entrance without wandering about). Where possible, specific times of opening are given in the individual entries, and also, where applicable, the nearest *vaporetto* to the church.

Essential Viewing

A detail from the exquisite mosaics in Basilica di S Marco

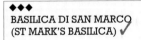

◆◆◆
BASILICA DI SAN MARCO (ST MARK'S BASILICA) ✓

Piazza San Marco
The cathedral of Venice evokes the blending of East and West that is at the heart of the Venetian character. More oriental than European, the architecture, the decoration and the atmosphere of ancient sanctity span both the centuries and the styles of Mediterranean civilisation. Originally built to house the body of St Mark, the patron saint of Venice, which had been smuggled from its

tomb in Alexandria by Venetians in AD 828, the basilica evolved its present appearance between the 9th and 19th centuries. The basic building dates from the late 11th century, the domes from the 13th and the decoration from subsequent centuries. Much of the decoration was plundered or presented to Venice during its time of supremacy, most notably the four famous gilded horses above the main doors. Made in the 4th century AD to surmount a Roman truimphal arch, they were looted from Constantinople, when it was sacked by the Venetians during the Crusades, and stood on the façade for nearly 600 years until plundered, in turn, by the French. After the Napoleonic wars, they were restored to the basilica although, because of atmospheric pollution, the originals are now kept in a gallery inside while replicas stand in their place.

The richness of ornament outside and inside the basilica can occupy hours but even the hurried visitor can admire the glowing gold of the mosaics which cover an acre of the vaulting, or examine them more closely from the galleries. The most famous single treasure of San Marco is the elaborate gold Byzantine altarpiece, the *Pala d'Oro*. Started in the 10th century, it was not completed until 1342. To see this and the treasury there is an entrance charge. *Open:* daily 09.45 to 17.00 hours Monday to Saturday, 14.00 to 17.00 hours Sunday (16.30 in winter).

Pala d'Oro and treasury are closed Sunday morning.

The Basilica has been the cathedral of Venice only since 1807. Before that time it had been the shrine of San Marco and the chapel of the Doge, while the church of San Pietro di Castello in the far east of the city (► 39) had been the cathedral, an arrangement to minimise the influence of the Papacy on the affairs of Venice.

There are two other churches, much larger than either of these, one to either side of the Grand Canal. The survival of both colossal buildings bears testimony to the strength of the city's medieval foundations

The usual crowds gathered in front of Basilica S Marco

laid in the mud of the lagoon islands.

◆◆◆
MIRACOLI (SANTA MARIA DEI MIRACOLI) ✔

Campo dei Miracoli, Cannaregio
One of the most exquisite small buildings in Venice, this church has often been described as looking like a jewel-box. Built in the 15th century of softly

coloured marble, it stands beside a canal with such elegance that its design needs no embellishment to satisfy the eye. When closed, the outer doors are often left open so that the interior, which is as lovely as the exterior, can be admired through an inner glass door.

◆◆◆
SANTI GIOVANNI E PAOLO (ST JOHN AND ST PAUL)
Campo Santi Giovanni e Paolo, Castello
Called San Zanipolo by Venetians, the church stands to the north of San Marco. The largest church in Venice, it was built by the Dominicans in the 14th and 15th centuries. Despite its bulk, the red brick building is not ponderous, partly because of the recent cleaning of the elaborate Gothic portals at the west end and the monuments within. Inside, the original choir screen and stalls have not survived, leaving the nave light and airy. The church is commonly called the Pantheon of Doges, and around the walls

27

stand magnificent monuments to Doges and, amongst other notables, the Venetian general Marcantonio Bragadin, who was flayed alive by the Turks when they captured Cyprus in 1571. Not only does a fresco on the monument depict this, but the flayed skin, which was stolen from Constantinople, lies in a small sarcophagus. His death was avenged at the Battle of Lepanto by Doge Sebastiano Venier, whose fine bronze statue also stands in the church.
Open: 07.30 to 12.30 and 15.00 to 19.00 hours.
Vaporetto: Ospedale Civile.

Red brick Basilica SS Giovanni e Paolo, the city's largest church

◆◆◆
SANTA MARIA GLORIOSA DEI FRARI (THE FRARI) ✓

Campo dei Frari, San Polo
This church stands on the far side of the Canal Grande. It is almost as large as Santi Giovanni e Paolo but has a wholly different character. The choir screen and stalls remain in place and the nave is shadowed and sombre, as are the vast and elaborate monuments. Memorable among these is the open-doored pyramid containing the heart of the centurysculptor Antonio Canova. He designed it as a monument to the great Venetian painter Titian, who, in fact, is

buried across the aisle under a dramatic 19th-century statue. Two paintings are the particular glories of the Frari. One is Titian's huge *The Assumption*, still in the position for which it was painted above the high altar. The other is *The Madonna and Child* by Bellini in the sacristy, one of the loveliest paintings in Venice.

Like San Zanipolo (► 27), the Frari can easily occupy an hour or more for those with a particular interest in painting, sculpture and architecture.
Open: 09.00 to 12.00 and 14.30 to 18.00 hours Monday to Saturday; 15.00 to 18.00 hours, Sunday (slightly reduced hours in winter).
Entrance charge.
Vaporetto: San Tomà.

Other Churches

A selection of churches is listed alphabetically below.

◆
ANGELO RAFFAELE

Campo Angelo Raffaele, Dorsoduro
This is a large church in need of restoration in a poor district towards the docks, but notable for its 18th-century organ decorated with charming paintings by Guardi.
Vaporetto: San Basilio.

◆
CARMINI (SANTA MARIA DEL CARMELO)

Campo Carmini, Dorsoduro
Near the Campo Santa Margherita, this is a large, sombre church displaying many fine paintings, including a series in the nave illustrating

the history of the Carmelite Order.
Vaporetto: Ca' Rezzonico.

◆
GESUATI (SANTA MARIA DEL ROSARIO)

Fondamenta delle Zattere, Dorsoduro
This is a surprisingly large church, its white and grey stone interior enlivened by the colour and zest of ceiling and altar paintings by Tiepolo.
Vaporetto: Zattere.

◆◆
GESUITI (SANTA MARIA ASSUNTA)

Campo dei Gesuiti, Cannaregio
The early 18th-century Jesuits built their church to impress, and the statuary along the skyline of its pediment gives a hint of what is within. Inside, the pillars and floor seem to be hung with green and white damask silk, which is also draped and ruffled around the pulpit on the north wall; but it all turns out to be marble.
Vaporetto: Fondamenta Nuove.

◆
GIGLIO (SANTA MARIA DEL GIGLIO)

Campo Santa Maria Zobenigo, San Marco
This appears the most worldly church in Venice, because the carvings on its façade depict fortified cities and warships. These commemorate the naval and diplomatic career of Antonio Barbaro, whose family paid for the building of the façade as his monument. The interior contains paintings by Tintoretto.

The 'silk' drapes of Gesuiti are in reality made of marble

Vaporetto: Santa Maria del Giglio.

◆◆
MADONNA DELL' ORTO
Campo Madonna dell' Orto, Cannaregio
Isolated in the north of the city, the church is a good goal for a long walk. A huge, light, airy church reminiscent of San Zanipolo, it was magnificently restored after the flood of 1966 by funds raised in Britain. Tintoretto, who is buried in one of the side chapels, was a parishioner and painted a number of pictures for the church, including the enormous *The Last Judgement* and *The Adoration of the Golden Calf,* both in the chancel, two

paintings behind the high altar and the charming *The Presentation of the Virgin.*
Vaporetto: Madonna dell' Orto.

◆
OSPEDALETTO (SANTA MARIA DEI DERELITTI)
Calle Barbaria delle Tole (near San Zanipolo), Castello
This is one of the Venetian oddities. Built in the late 17th century, its façade is a sculptured riot of grotesque figures and its interior is cluttered with ornament and paintings of the 17th and 18th centuries.
Vaporetto: Ospedale Civile.

◆
PIETÀ
Riva degli Schiavoni, Castello
This has been used for concerts since the 17th century, and during the 18th century Vivaldi composed music for the choir. Music is still played here regularly on Monday evenings, when audiences can take the opportunity to admire the oval painting by Giambattista Tiepolo on the ceiling, *The Coronation of the Virgin.* The church is only opened for concerts.
Vaporetto: San Zaccaria.

◆
REDENTORE
Campo Redentore, Giudecca Island
This is best seen across the water from the centre of Venice. Indeed, its architect, Palladio, who was commissioned to design it as an act of thanksgiving for the ending of a 16th-century plague, intended it to catch and

hold the distant eye. The façade and the interior together form a magnificent example of what came to be known as Palladian architecture. On the third Sunday of July, a bridge of boats is constructed across the Giudecca Canal for the celebration of the Feast of the Redeemer (Redentore). The church is dramatically floodlit at night.
Vaporetto: Redentore.

◆◆◆
SALUTE (SANTA MARIA DELLA SALUTE)

Campo della Salute, Dorsoduro, near the eastern end of the Grand Canal
Like the Redentore this church was built to give thanks for the ending of a plague, but in the following century. The great domed church at the entrance to the Grand Canal has sometimes been seen as the hostess of the city, welcoming visitors; as the novelist Henry James wrote: 'like some great lady on the threshold of her salon … with her domes and scrolls, her scalloped buttresses and statues forming a pompous crown, and her wide steps disposed on the ground like the train of a robe'. After dark, a walk through the alleys of Dorsoduro can suddenly end on the brilliantly floodlit steps of the Salute beneath its gleaming bulk, the water below dancing with reflected light.
The magnificent baroque interior is decorated with paintings by Titian.
Vaporetto: Salute.

SANT' ALVISE
*Campo Sant' Alvise,
Cannaregio*

Although one of the most remote (and often shut) churches in the city, this is a useful destination for a long walk including the Madonna dell' Orto and the Ghetto (► 30 and 18). Its most notable painting (by Tiepolo) having been removed to the Accademia Gallery, the church's principal feature is now a spectacular but clumsily executed painted *trompe l'oeil* ceiling, depicting Heaven as seen from a grandiose courtyard – a somewhat cruder version of the extraordinary painted ceiling in San Pantalon (► 39).
Vaporetto: Sant' Alvise.

SANTI APOSTOLI
*Campo dei Santi Apostoli,
Cannaregio*

This church is worth visiting just for *The Communion of Santa Lucia* by the elder Tiepolo in the delightful 15th-century Corner family chapel. The exceptionally tall 17th-century campanile, crowned by an onion dome (which was added 50 years later) is a Venetian landmark.
Vaporetto: Ca' d'Oro.

SAN CASSIANO
Campo San Cassiano, San Polo

This sumptuous church, with its pillars draped in crimson, is worth visiting for Tintoretto's majestic *Crucifixion.*
Vaporetto: San Stae.

◆
SAN FRANCESCO DELLA VIGNA
*Campo della Confraternità,
Castello*

This is a large church in the less-visited northeast of the city near the Arsenale, and its huge campanile is sometimes mistaken for that of San Marco from a distance. It contains beautiful paintings – although none of the first rank – including

Salute at sunset, seen from the island of S Giorgio Maggiore

a delightful 15th-century
Madonna and Child Enthroned
by Antonio da Negroponte.
Vaporetto: Celestia.

◆
SAN GEREMIA E LUCIA
Campo San Geremia,
Cannaregio
Standing on the corner of the
Grand Canal and the Canale di
Cannaregio, this vast, light,
plain church is now remarkable
for housing the body of Santa
Lucia, which was removed from
her own church when it was
demolished to make way for

the railway station that was to
be named after her. Wearing a
gold mask and a red and gold
robe, she lies in a glass case.
Vaporetto: Ponte delle Guglie.

◆◆
SAN GIACOMO DELL' ORIO
Campo San Giacomo dell' Orio,
Santa Croce
A busy parish church in a quiet
campo in the west of the city,
where the only visitors are
likely to be those walking to the
Piazzale Roma to catch a bus.
Its styles of architecture and
decoration reflect the growth of

Venice: pillars from Byzantium and one of the two 'ship's keel' roofs (like an inverted wooden ship) in Venice – the other is in Santo Stefano; paintings by Venetian masters, including Veronese; and, in comic contrast, a funny little relief carving of a knight – almost a cartoon character – on the outside wall.

Vaporetto: San Stae or Riva di Biasio.

◆

SAN GIACOMO DI RIALTO

Campo San Giacomo, San Polo
It stands among the fruit and vegetable market stalls at the foot of the Rialto Bridge. The oldest church in the city – said to have been founded in the early 5th century – it has grown many architectural and decorative curiosities, including a rare brick dome, over-large baroque altarpieces and, most notably, a large, 15th-century 24-hour clock on the façade. It faces the market square, which was once used by Venetian bankers, money-changers and insurance brokers – including, presumably, Shakespeare's Shylock.

Vaporetto: Rialto.

◆

SAN GIOBBE

Campo San Giobbe, Cannaregio
Another remote church to the northwest of the city, it is often locked. Suffering from damp and in need of restoration, it is worth a visit to see those of its paintings that have not been removed to the Accademia Gallery, including a triptych by Antonio Vivarini.

Vaporetto: Ponte dei Tre Archi.

◆

SAN GIORGIO DEI GRECI

Fondamenta dei Greci, Castello
The church is quickly recognisable by its dangerously tilted 16th-century campanile, caused by gradual subsidence. The church of the Greek community – many of whom were refugees from Constantinople when it was taken by the Turks in the 15th century – its decoration is strongly Byzantine and Greek Orthodox.

Vaporetto: San Zaccaria.

SAN GIORGIO MAGGIORE

Campo San Giorgio, Isola San Giorgio Maggiore
The church stands on its island across the Basin of San Marco, giving Venice one of its most celebrated views. Designed by Andrea Palladio in the 16th century, it has all the majesty that the term 'Palladian' implies and this is particularly apparent at night when the façade is floodlit. The interior is vast and austere, its white stone a magnificent setting for its works of art, including paintings by Tintoretto and a bronze altarpiece, *The Globe Surmounted by God the Father,* dating from the 16th century.

The tall campanile, ascended by a lift, offers the best bird's-eye views of Venice because, unlike that of San Marco, it is detached from the city which can therefore be seen as a panorama across the water.

Vaporetto: San Giorgio.

After the daily fruit and vegetable market outside S Giacomo di Rialto – the oldest church in Venice

◆◆
SAN GIOVANNI IN BRAGORA
Campo Bandiera e Moro, Castello
This fascinating little parish church, where Antonio Vivaldi was baptised, lies hidden in a quiet *campo* off the Riva degli Schiavoni. Among its paintings is a lovely, peaceful *Madonna and Child with Saints* by Bartolomeo Vivarini.
Vaporetto: Arsenale.

◆
SAN GIOVANNI CRISOSTOMO
Campo San Giovanni Crisosotomo, Cannaregio
A small, busy, very Venetian parish church. Richly decorated, it is remarkable for a lovely painting of saints by Giovanni Bellini.
Vaporetto: Rialto.

◆◆
SAN GIULIANO
Campo San Zulian, San Marco
Known by Venetians as San Zulian, it is in the midst of busy

35

Don't miss a trip to the romantic island of S Giorgio Maggiore – celebrated for the views from its church tower

shopping alleys, just north of the Piazza San Marco.
The interior is opulent and very Venetian. Golden cherubs hold a draped red backcloth behind the gilded and richly decorated high altar, and the ceiling is painted with the familiar and spectacular Venetian view of heaven from earth.
Vaporetto: San Marco.

SANTA MARIA ASSUNTA *see* **GESUITI**

SANTA MARIA DEL CARMELO *see* **CARMINI**

SANTA MARIA DEI DERELITTI *see* **OSPEDALETTO**

◆
SANTA MARIA DELLA FAVA
Campo della Fava, San Marco
Named 'St Mary of the Bean' after a popular cake (called *fave dolce,* sweet beans) once produced by a nearby bakery, this church is also known as

Santa Maria della Consolazione. It is a high-ceilinged 18th-century church decorated in grey statuary by Bernardi, the teacher of Canova, and a lovely early painting by Tiepolo, *The Education of the Virgin*. *Vaporetto:* Rialto.

SANTA MARIA DEL GIGLIO
see **GIGLIO**

SANTA MARIA DEI MIRACOLI
see **MIRACOLI**

SANTA MARIA DI NAZARETH
see **SCALZI**

SANTA MARIA DEL ROSARIO
see **GESUATI**

SANTA MARIA DELLA SALUTE *see* **SALUTE**

◆
SANTA MARIA FORMOSA
Campo Santa Maria Formosa, Castello
The 15th-century church dominates a large square enlivened by cafés and market stalls. It is filled with interesting monuments and paintings, including works by Vivarini (*The Madonna of Mercy)* and Palma il Vecchio (*The Martyrdom of St Barbara*). Outside, at the base of the campanile, is the carved stone mask of a bearded man 'leering in brutal degradation', as described by the art historian John Ruskin, who could hardly bring himself to look at it.

◆◆
SAN MARTINO
Campo San Martino, Castello
This is a lovely, little-visited church near the Arsenale, and it is probable that the wooden angels and cherubs around the organ were carved by craftsmen who decorated the great galleys in the dockyard. It has another spectacular ceiling painted with an *Ascension into Heaven*, past the pillars of an atrium, that seems to grow out of the architecture. The profusion of monuments and paintings makes this a very Venetian church, and outside in the wall is one of the now-rare 'lion's mask' letterboxes for notes denouncing enemies of the state.
Vaporetto: Arsenale.

The vast, cool interior of Palladio's S Giorgio Maggiore

SAN MAURIZIO
Campo San Maurizio, San Marco
This faces the square on the well-trodden route between San Marco and the Accademia Bridge, where antiques markets are occasionally held. Originally an ancient church, it was completely rebuilt in 1806 when Venice was under French rule and so is often ignored by admirers of the Venetian Republic. It is a handsome, plain church in neoclassical style, its cool and elegant interior given a dramatic focal point by the white marble tabernacle on the high altar, thrown into

relief by the red drapery behind, held by gilded cherubs above.

SAN MOISÈ
Campo San Moisè, San Marco
The over-elaborate baroque façade of San Moisè, described as the clumsiest church in Venice, commands the attention of those walking towards San Marco from the Accademia bridge. Its interior is just as odd: the high altar appears at first sight to be a bizarre rockery but turns out to be a tableau of *Moses on Mount Sinai Receiving the Tablets*. The building is in startling contrast to the smooth, smart looks of the Hotel Bauer Grünwald next door.
Vaporetto: San Marco.

SAN NICOLÒ DEI MENDICOLI

Campo San Nicolò, Dorsoduro
This ornate yet modest parish church in a poor district of the city near the docks is one of Venice's oldest churches. Restored by British contributions to the Venice in Peril Fund in 1977, its gilded wooden statues gleam anew. Built between the 12th and 15th centuries and well-stocked with statuary and paintings, it is a good goal when exploring the hinterland of the western end of the Zattere and visiting the nearby churches of San Sebastiano and Angelo Raffaele.
Vaporetto: San Basilio.

◆

SAN NICOLÒ DA TOLENTINI

Campo dei Tolentini, Santa Croce
This colossal church with a vast, pillared Corinthian portico is close to the Piazzale Roma and the car parks, and so is popular for weddings. Embedded in the façade (under the porch) you can see a cannon ball, left by the Austrians during the siege of 1849. Inside, it is elaborate, enriched with sculpture and paintings.
Vaporetto: Piazzale Roma.

◆◆◆

SAN PANTALÒN

Campo San Pantalòn, Dorsoduro
This typically Venetian baroque church probably makes a more immediate impact on the visitor than any church in Venice. On entering

and looking up, the vast flat ceiling can be seen to be one enormous view of a mass ascent into Heaven. This startling scene also includes the life and martyrdom of San Pantalòn and was painted at the end of the 17th century and the beginning of the 18th. A typically quirky Venetian postscript is the fate of the artist, Gian Antonio Fumiani, who, as he completed his work, stepped back to admire it better, fell from the scaffolding to his death and was buried in the church he had decorated so memorably. The church also contains smaller works by Veronese and Vivarini. Like several other Venetian churches, it has no façade as its builders ran out of money.
Vaporetto: San Tomà.

◆

SAN PIETRO DI CASTELLO

Campo San Pietro, Isola di San Pietro
As it stands forlornly on its little island at the far eastern extremity of Venice, the church seems to be dreaming of past glories. This was the first of the central Venetian islands to be settled, and the church became the cathedral of Venice in AD 775, remaining so until 1807, when the Basilica di San Marco, formerly the Doges' private chapel, took its place. Its isolation here throughout the life of the Venetian Republic was a deliberate attempt to minimise the influence of the Pope and Rome. It overlooks a usually deserted stretch of grass and

trees. Inside, the church, which was built to a Palladian design in the 16th century to replace its predecessors, is lofty and rather grand but, above all, neglected.
Vaporetto: Giardini.

SAN POLO
Campo San Polo, San Polo
The church stands in the largest square in the city after San Marco. Its works of art include fine bronze statues of saints on the high altar and notable paintings by Tintoretto and both Tiepolos, including 18 paintings of *The Stations of the Cross* by the younger.
Vaporetto: San Tomà.

SAN ROCCO
Campo San Rocco, San Polo
Standing beside the famous *scuola* (► 45), it is chiefly remarkable for large paintings of the saint's miracles by Tintoretto.
Vaporetto: San Tomà.

◆◆
SAN SALVATORE
Campo San Salvador, San Marco
This is regarded as one of the finest Renaissance churches in Italy. Principally admired for its architecture, its works of art include a painting by Titian of *The Annunciation*.
Vaporetto: Rialto.

SAN SEBASTIANO
Campo San Sebastiano, Dorsoduro
The most important of the three major churches near the

docks, it belongs to the great painter Paolo Veronese, who decorated it and is buried there. His works are everywhere in the church, including the open doors of the organ and the ceiling, in the chancel, the sacristy and the gallery, where he painted frescoes on the walls. In all, he painted here the richest and most comprehensive exhibition of his own work and one that no admirer of Venetian art should miss. Sadly, opening times of the church are unpredictable and it has recently been closed for long-term restoration. Check with the tourist office as to its opening times.
Vaporetto: San Basilio.

SAN STAE
Campo San Stae, Canal Grande, Santa Croce
Despite its handsome interior, this church is at its best viewed from the outside. Its neoclassical façade, decorated with joyous baroque statuary, provides one of the most striking views on the Grand Canal. The interior is used for art exhibitions. The beautiful little goldsmiths' *scuola* that adjoins it – one of the prettiest buildings in Venice – is now sadly empty and virtually derelict.
Vaporetto: San Stae.

SANTO STEFANO
Campo Francesco Morosini, San Marco
A large, handsome church with one of only two 'ship's keel' roofs – like a huge, inverted

wooden hull – in the city (the other is in San Giacomo dell'Orio). Richly painted and decorated with inlaid, multi-coloured marble, the church contains paintings by Tintoretto. Outside are cloisters and a leaning 16th-century campanile.
Vaporetto: Accademia or Sant' Angelo.

◆
SAN TROVASO
Campo San Trovaso, Dorsoduro
This is a huge Palladian church with two identical façades because, it is said, two rival 16th-century families each wanted to be the first to enter and so could do so simultaneously. The interior is lofty, light and peaceful; outside, the *campo* in front of the two main doors is a good

S Zaccaria displays fine paintings

place to sit in the sun away from the city bustle.
Vaporetto: Zattere.

◆◆◆
SAN ZACCARIA
Campo San Zaccaria, Castello
The massive 16th-century church – with traces of its predecessors – is filled with paintings. The most celebrated of these is Bellini's *Madonna and Child with Saints* in the north aisle. During the Venetian Republic, the nunnery attached to the church was favoured by rich families as a refuge for their unattached daughters. There is also a waterlogged crypt where several Doges are interred (entrance charge).
Vaporetto: San Zaccaria.

◆◆
SCALZI (SANTA MARIA DI NAZARETH)
Fondamenta Scalzi, Cannaregio
Close to the railway station, the

church is well placed for those wanting a first, or last, look at something intensely Venetian. The *scalzi* were 'barefooted' Carmelite friars who came here in the mid-17th century and commissioned the church. The ornate baroque façade is an indication of the sumptuous but gloomy interior of multi-coloured marble, statuary and 18th-century paintings. Appropriately, the last of the Doges, Ludovico Manin, is buried there.
Vaporetto: Ferrovia.

Landmarks
Despite first impressions, many of the most celebrated buildings in Venice are in fact neither churches nor palaces but those built for a specific purpose in the everyday life of the city.

◆
ARSENALE
The naval power-house of the Venetian Empire was the *Arsenale,* the great dockyard in the east of the city. Surrounded by 15th-century castellated walls and entered through a monumental archway and watergate, it was where the galleys that conquered the Mediterranean and dominated it for centuries were built and based. The interior is now mostly deserted dockside and bare walls, but the gates – guarded by stone lions brought from Greece in the 17th and 18th centuries – can easily be admired from the *campiello* outside.
Vaporetto: Arsenale.

The entrance to the Arsenale – where the great ships of the Venetian Empire were built and berthed

◆◆◆
CAMPANILE DI SAN MARCO (ST MARK'S BELL TOWER)
The tower rises 325 feet (99m) above the piazza, the tallest building in Venice. The original collapsed in 1902 but was rebuilt over the next 10 years. It is entered through the beautiful little *loggetta,* built in the 16th century by Jacopo Sansovino and restored after it was

destroyed by the collapsing campanile. An internal lift takes visitors to the gallery surrounding the belfry, which commands panoramic views of the city, the lagoon and, on clear days, the Veneto and the Alps.
Open: daily, 09.30 to 17.30 hours.
Entrance charge.

◆◆◆
DOGANA DI MARE (CUSTOMS HOUSE)
This stands where the Dorsoduro district of Venice (to the east of the church of the Salute) juts out like a ship's prow into the lagoon at the junction of the Canal Grande and the Basin of San Marco. On top of its tower stand two bronze figures of Atlas holding up a golden globe surmounted by a figure of Fortune as a wind-vane. Behind the tower are the 17th-century Customs warehouses. You can stop for a moment and enjoy the views to St Mark's and over the lagoon. Closed to the public except during exhibitions.
Vaporetto: Salute.

◆◆◆
PONTE DI RIALTO (RIALTO BRIDGE)

Built of Istrian stone in the late 16th century this was, until 1854, the only crossing of the Grand Canal and replaced a wooden bridge. A single span, decorated with relief carvings and balustrades, it is famous for its parallel rows of shops facing one another to either side of the central path. These sell mostly jewellery, leather goods, silk and shoes. The bridge commands fine views of the Grand Canal, particularly in the direction of San Marco.
Vaporetto: Rialto.

Shoes for the well-heeled are for sale on the Ponte di Rialto

◆◆◆
SQUERO DI SAN TROVASO
on the San Trovaso Canal (near the Zattere), Dorsoduro
This is a picturesque boatyard where gondolas have been built and repaired for hundreds of years. Even though it is closed to the public you can get great photographs of the upturned gondolas awaiting repair, with the church of San Trovaso as a backdrop, all from the opposite side of the canal. Not open to the public.
Vaporetto: Zattere.

◆◆◆
TEATRO LA FENICE
Campo San Fantin, San Marco
Spare a thought for this tragic building site as you pass by, for this is where the famous early 19th-century opera house of

Venice, one of the oldest and most beautiful theatres of Europe, once stood. It was utterly destroyed by fire on 29 January 1996. More than a year later two electricians were sentenced for arson. The building will eventually be reconstructed but, as you will see, progress is slow. In the meantime La Fenice opera company is still operating from a marquee (the Palafenice) on Tronchetto, one of the islands in the lagoon. All proceeds from the concerts and winter opera series go towards the restoration fund. Contact 041 5210161 for further information.

◆◆◆
TORRE DELL'OROLOGIO (CLOCK TOWER)
Piazza San Marco
The tower stands above the arch leading to the Mercerie shopping street close to the Basilica San Marco. Built at the end of the 15th century, its remarkable, brightly-enamelled clock-face and its digital clock are linked with automata, which attract crowds in the Piazza. On the summit of the tower two large bronze figures known as the *Mori* (Moors) strike the hour. During Ascension Week and at Epiphany, figures of the Magi emerge to either side of the clock-face and bow to the statue of the Madonna above it. Unfortunately, the Clock Tower has been closed to the public for several years for restoration purposes. The authorities hope that it will reopen soon. Check with the tourist office in Venice for the current position.

Scuole
The *scuole* of Venice were 'fraternity houses', where the more prosperous Venetians organised the city's welfare and administered charities. Many became elaborate treasure-houses of the arts and still contain some of the most remarkable collections of paintings in Venice, which reflects their prestige.

◆◆
SCUOLA GRANDE DEI CARMINI
Campo dei Carmini (near Campo Santa Margherita beside the Carmelites' church), Dorsoduro
The Carmini had Giambattista Tiepolo (the elder) as its principal decorator in the 18th century. Although the themes are, as usual, religious, his painting is sensual and so suited the mood of his time.
Open: 09.00 to 12.00 and 15.00 to 18.00 hours, Monday to Saturday.
Entrance charge.
Vaporetto: Ca' Rezzonico.

◆◆◆
SCUOLA GRANDE DI SAN ROCCO ✓
Campo San Rocco, San Polo
This is the largest and grandest of the *scuole*, standing close to the church of the Frari. It is most celebrated for its great series of powerful paintings by Tintoretto depicting Biblical scenes. The whole interior is richly decorated, carved and gilded.
Open: daily 09.00 to 17.30 hours (10.00 to 16.00 hours in winter).
Entrance charge.
Vaporetto: San Tomà.

♦♦♦
SCUOLA DI SAN GIORGIO DEGLI SCHIAVONI

Calle Furlani, Castello
This has the early 16th-century artist Vittore Carpaccio's paintings as its main attraction. Downstairs in the little *scuola,* he painted an enchanting frieze illustrating the lives of three saints, St George, St Jerome and St Tryphon. There is also a painting of St Augustine in his study – an intimate glimpse into a medieval Venetian room.
Open: 10.00 to 12.30 and 15.00 to 18.00 hours, Tuesday to Sunday. Closed on Monday. Entrance charge.
Vaporetto: San Zaccaria.

Two magnificent *scuole* – **San Giovanni Evangelista,** Campiello de la Scuola, San Polo, and **San Marco**, Campo San Giovanni e Paolo, Castello – are not generally open to the public but have splendid exteriors. The former, which is near the Frari, is approached through a beautiful marble arched screen; its interior is remarkable for a converging double staircase. Admission is possible when exhibitions are held, or sometimes on request. The latter, standing next to the church of San Zanipolo, now houses the main hospital and can be visited by appointment. However, its most interesting works of art, relief carvings incorporating startling perspectives, can be seen on the outside wall facing the *campo.*

Museums and Galleries

♦♦♦
ACCADEMIA
Campo della Carità, Dorsoduro
The most famous and comprehensive collection of Venetian painting is housed in this former church, monastery and *scuola* at the Dorsoduro side of the wooden Accademia Bridge (one of the three crossing points of the Canal Grande). Most of the paintings come from palaces and churches in the city and, although it would have been more appropriate to see them in their original settings, here they are grouped in galleries and are well lit.
Usually some galleries are closed for various reasons, but there is always enough on display to delight and even sometimes to cause visual and mental indigestion. Highlights include Giovanni Bellini's *Madonna Enthroned* and Carpaccio's *The Presentation of Jesus* in Room II, Giorgione's *Tempest* and Bellini's *Madonna of the Trees* in Room V; Titian's *St John the Baptist* in Room VI; three magnificent paintings by Veronese in Room XI; the Accademia's only Canaletto and six charming 18th-century *Scenes from Venetian Life* by Longhi in Room XVII; and Carpaccio's enchanting series of paintings illustrating *The Legend of St Ursula,* portraying the clothes and settings of 15th-century Venice, in Room XXI.
Open: daily, 09.00 to 19.00

A detail from Carpaccio's epic St Ursula *in the Accademia*

hours. However, the daily allocation of tickets are sold early in the day.
Entrance charge.
For information telephone 041 5222247.
Vaporetto: Accademia.

◆◆
CA' D'ORO GALLERIA FRANCHETTI (FRANCHETTI GALLERY)

Grand Canal, Cannaregio 3922
The 'House of Gold', the most famous *palazzo* on the Grand Canal, was named after the gilding on its elaborate façade when it was new. The façade, however, is no longer gleaming

47

Although no longer gilded, the Ca' d'Oro remains a magnificent example of Venetian architecture

and golden and, whilst undergoing major restoration, it lacks its original sumptuous ornamentation. Inside the *palazzo* an elegant new gallery displays Italian art, including frescoes by Titian and Giorgione. Reopened in 1984, this magnificent building retains its architectural bones, but sadly not its atmosphere of former grandeur.
Open: daily, 09.00 to 14.00 hours.

Entrance charge.
For information call 041 5238790.
Vaporetto: Ca' d'Oro.

◆
CA' PESARO GALLERIA D'ARTE MODERNA E MUSEO ORIENTALE (GALLERY OF MODERN ART AND ORIENTAL MUSEUM)
Canal Grande, Santa Croce
Worth visiting if only to see inside this enormous 17th-century baroque *palazzo* overlooking the Grand Canal. It was built for Giovanni Pesaro, who became Doge in 1658. It

◆◆◆
CA' REZZONICO MUSEO DEL SETTECENTO VENEZIANO (MUSEUM OF EIGHTEENTH-CENTURY VENICE) ✓

Grand Canal, Dorsoduro
This immensely grand 17th-century palace overlooking the Grand Canal has been filled with furniture and paintings of the 18th century. The magnificent rooms of the *piano nobile* are richly decorated with gilding, frescoes and painted ceilings, including one by Tiepolo. On the floor above can be seen paintings of Venetian life by Guardi and Longhi, and a succession of small rooms, decorated with frescoes by the younger Tiepolo. The top floor, which houses a collection of costumes, the stock of a pharmacist's shop and a marionette theatre, is often closed.
The poet Robert Browning occupied a suite of rooms below the *piano nobile* (not open to the public) from 1888 until his death here in 1889.
Open: 10.00 to 17.00 hours (16.00 hours in winter), Saturday to Thursday; closed Friday.
Entrance charge.
Vaporetto: Ca' Rezzonico.

◆◆◆
COLLEZIONE (RACOLTA) GUGGENHEIM (GUGGENHEIM COLLECTION)
Calle San Cristoforo, Dorsoduro 701
The collection of Cubist, Abstract and Surrealist art

houses contemporary art exhibitions on the first two floors and oriental art on the top floor. The Museo Orientale is a treasure trove of artifacts collected by Conti di Bardi during a lengthy voyage to the Far East in the 19th century. The Museo d'Arte Moderna began with a handful of pieces bought from the Biennale, and now contains works by such artists as Matisse, Miró and Klee.
Open: 09.00 to 19.00 hours, Tuesday to Sunday.
Entrance charge.
Vaporetto: San Stae.

acquired by the late Peggy Guggenheim, the American millionairess, is housed in her former home, an unfinished 18th-century *palazzo* on the Canal Grande, Palazzo Venier de Leoni. Paintings and sculptures of the 20th century – including Peggy Guggenheim's own discovery, Jackson Pollock – will delight those who appreciate modern art, while those who do not will enjoy the view from the garden, overlooking the Grand Canal. *Open:* 11.00 to 18.00 hours, Wednesday to Monday; closed on Tuesday.
Entrance charge.
For further information telephone 041 5206288.
Vaporetto: Accademia or Salute.

FORTUNY MUSEUM *see* **MUSEO FORTUNY**

FRANCHETTI GALLERY *see* **CA' D'ORO**

GUGGENHEIM COLLECTION *see* **COLLEZIONE GUGGENHEIM**

◆

MUSEO ARCHEOLOGICO (ARCHAEOLOGICAL MUSEUM)
Piazzetta San Marco 17, San Marco
The museum contains a collection of original Greek and Roman sculpture, much of

'The Angel of the Citadel', one of the startling pieces in the Guggenheim Collection

which was bought together in the 16th century. It is temporarily housed in the Procuratie Nuove, which adjoins the Marciana Library (closed to the public except the reading-room, which can be visited by telephoned application to 041 2407211).
Open: daily 09.00 to 14.00 hours.
Entrance charge.
For further information telephone 041 5225978.
Vaporetto: San Marco.

♦♦
MUSEO CORRER (CORRER MUSEUM)
Piazza San Marco, San Marco
The principal historical museum of the city runs above the Procuratie Nuove arcade on the west and south sides of the Piazza and is entered by a wide marble staircase at the western end. The exhibits include paintings, models, costumes, books, arms and armour, much of it captured from the Turks. Particularly sinister is the lion's mask letter-box (*bocca di leone*) for written denunciations of enemies of the state. There are also relics of the *Bucintoro*, the huge, elaborate ceremonial galley used by the Doges.
Open: daily, 07.00 to 19.00 hours (17.00 hours in winter).
Entrance charge.
For further information telephone 041 5225625.
Vaporetto: San Marco.

♦
MUSEO DIOCESANO DI ARTE SACRA
Ponte della Canonica, Castello
This tiny but extraordinary museum is a storeroom and restoration centre for works of art from local churches and monasteries. Some are stolen works of art that have been retrieved by the police.
Open: 10.30 to 12.30 hours, Monday to Saturday.
Entrance charge.
For further information telephone 041 5229166.
Vaporetto: San Zaccaria.

♦♦
MUSEO FORTUNY (FORTUNY MUSEUM)
Campo San Benedetto, San Marco
The Palazzo Pesaro degli Orfei was the home and studio of the Spanish-born artist, sculptor, architect and dress-designer Mariano Fortuny (1871–1949). His studio contains a permanent exhibition of his work and is redolent of rich bohemian life in Venice at the turn of the century. Temporary exhibitions are also held in the 15th-century *palazzo,* which was bequeathed to the city by Fortuny's widow.
Open: daily except Monday, 09.00 to 19.00 hours.
Entrance charge.
For further information telephone 041 5200995
Vaporetto: San Angelo.

♦
MUSEO QUERINI-STAMPALIA
Campiello Querini, Castello
The Querini-Stampalia *palazzo* was the home of another grand Venetian family and 20 rooms are still furnished with their splendid collection of pictures and furniture. Certain exhibits may even be borrowed. This and the Palazzo Mocenigo are

Detail of a model of a ceremonial barge on display in the Museo Storico Navale

two of many such palaces, illustrating the extraordinary richness of Venice at the height of its power.
Open: 10.00 to 13.00 and 15.00 to 18.00 hours, Tuesday to Thursday and Sunday; 10.00 to 13.00 and 15.00 to 22.00 hours Friday and Saturday; closed Monday. Entrance charge.
For further information telephone 041 2711411.
Vaporetto: San Zaccharia.

◆◆
MUSEO STORICO NAVALE (NAVAL MUSEUM)
Campo San Biagio, Castello
The museum records the

illustrious maritime past of Venice with a magnificent collection of ship models, pictures and relics housed in an old granary near the Arsenale, which was the naval base of the Republic (➤ 42). The exhibits range from models of the galleys that fought the corsairs and Turks to the human torpedoes used in World War II. There is a special section devoted to the gondola and other Venetian craft, with actual boats displayed in part of the Arsenale itself.
Open: daily, 08.45 to 13.30 hours, Monday to Saturday; closed Sunday.
Entrance charge.
For further information telephone 041 5200276.
Vaporetto: Arsenale.

NAVAL MUSEUM *see* MUSEO STORICO NAVALE

◆◆
PALAZZO MOCENIGO (MOCENIGO PALACE)
Salizzada San Stae, Santa Croce 1992
This was the home of one of the oldest and grandest Venetian families until recent years. The nine elegantly furnished rooms of the 17th-century *palazzo* provide a rare insight into 18th-century Venetian noble life. Richly gilded and painted, these rooms, with their fine furniture and Murano glass chandeliers, still have a private feeling about them. The building also houses a library and a collection of period costume, and there is also a small exhibition of antique Venetian textiles.
Open: 08.30 to 13.30 hours, Monday to Saturday.

Entrance charge.
For further information
telephone 041 721798
Vaporetto: San Stae.

EXCURSIONS FROM VENICE (VENÉZIA)

Islands

Scattered across nearly 200 square miles (500 sq km) of the Venetian lagoon are some 40 islands. Half of them are now deserted, while those still inhabited may be thriving communities or isolated institutions – a prison, a hospital or a religious retreat – and a few are used for public or private recreation. Enough of them can be visited to add another dimension to a holiday

Lace-making in Burano is an ancient art still plied by the women of the island, who can be seen at work

53

in Venice. The main islands are well-serviced by *vaporetto*, but the others can only be reached by water-taxi.

◆◆◆
BURANO

The fishermen's and lace-makers' island with a population of about 5,000, lies more than five miles (8km) to the northeast of Venice. While Murano (► 56) is workaday and slightly dishevelled, Burano is neat and clean and its multi-coloured cottages lining little canals make it a perfect subject for photographs. Its character has been shaped by its industries – the robust way of life of its fishermen and boat-builders and the delicacy of its lace-makers' skills. Usually women can be seen making lace

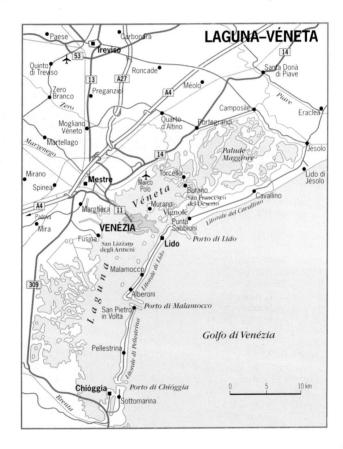

LAGUNA–VÉNETA

54

outside the doors of their cottages – although they are now dwindling in number – and their products (as well as embroidery from Hong Kong) are on sale at stalls and local shops.

There are few buildings of note but the church of **San Martino** contains a painting of *The Crucifixion* by the elder Tiepolo and boasts the most alarmingly tilted campanile of them all.

Vaporetto: route 12.

◆◆
CHIOGGIA

Once an island, Chioggia is now, like Venice, connected to the mainland by a causeway; unlike Venice, several of its canals have been filled in to become roads for cars. In the far south of the lagoon, 16 miles (25.5km) from Venice, it has grown from a fishing-port to an important town of some 55,000 inhabitants. Now, in essence, it belongs to the mainland rather than the lagoon.

Much of the town, particularly around the remaining canals, is reminiscent of Venice and many buildings date from the 13th to 18th centuries. There are several fine churches, notably the **Duomo**, built between the 13th and 17th centuries, which contains a painting by the elder Tiepolo. There are a number of excellent fish restaurants near the harbour and in the Corso del Popolo.

Vaporetto: route 11 from the Lido (or by bus from the Piazzale Roma).

The colours of Burano could have come straight from the set of an Italian opera

◆◆
THE LIDO

This is the only one of the Venetian islands to have roads, and its buses, cars and lorries are imported by ferry from the mainland. A little to the southeast of Venice, it is just over seven miles (11km) long and half a mile (1km) wide, covering the largest sand bank between the lagoon and the Adriatic. With a population of about 20,000 it is essentially a seaside holiday resort and is crowded in summer, when it is also host to the International Film Festival.

It was at its most fashionable before World War I as the architecture of its hotels and villas testifies, and its long sandy beach is still lined with wooden bathing-huts, which recall that time. Its most notable building is, in fact, a short distance across the water: the 16th-century **fortress of Sant' Andrea**, built on the little island of Vignole to command the main entrance to the lagoon. It was the guns of this fort that fired on a French warship in 1797, so precipitating the French invasion and the end of the Republic. The fortress, adorned with a massive relief carving of the Lion of St Mark, is currently under major restoration and not open to the public.

From the *vaporetto* bound from the Lido to San Marco, Venice is seen as it was intended it should first be seen, from the deck of a ship approaching from the sea, its towers, domes and palaces materialising between water and sky in one of the great spectacles the world has to offer.

Vaporetto: routes 1, 6, 14, 52, 61 and 82 (route 6 is the quickest, taking just 10 minutes); route 62 serves the Casino.

From the *vaporetto* landing stage of *Santa Maria Elizabetta*, ACTV buses leave for all destinations on the Lido. *Linea A* goes to the north, to the public bathing beaches and to the Casino; *Linea B* goes to the beaches and also south to the golf course at Alberoni; while

The island of Murano is famous for its glass, but another attraction is S Donato and its elegant clocktower

Linea 11 also heads southwards and to the main beaches.

MURANO

With a population of nearly 8,000, Murano lies a short distance to the north of the city. It is an industrial island and has

the feel of a small working town, although some of its factories lie derelict. Glass is its product and has been since the 13th century, when production was moved out of Venice itself because of the fire-risk. Venetian glass has long been a curious mixture of the beautiful and the vulgar, whether in table-glass, ornaments, mirrors or chandeliers.

Past products can be seen in the **Museo Vetrario di Murano**, in Palazzo Giustinian, Fondamenta Giustinian and Fondamenta Manin (tel: 041 739586).

Open: 10.00 to 17.00 hours (16.00 hours in winter), Thursday to Tuesday; closed Wednesday.

Entrance charge.

New production can be seen in many factory showrooms to which visitors will constantly be invited.

Murano is a miniature, shabbier Venice with its own scaled-down Canal Grande, crossed by a single bridge. Its most notable building is the church of **Santi Maria e Donato,** which has a 12th-century mosaic floor and a 15th-century 'ship's keel' roof. *Vaporetto:* routes 12, 14 and 52.

◆
SAN FRANCESCO DEL DESERTO
This remote and peaceful island can be reached by ferry from Burano and the resident friars will show visitors the 13th-century cloister and the church of the hermitage, where St Francis of Assisi is said to have stayed.
Open: daily 09.30 to 11.30 hours and 15.00 to 17.00 hours. Donation on admission. Access is from Burano, by water-taxi.

◆
SAN LAZZARO DEGLI ARMENI
This Armenian island can also be visited to see the church, library and monastery where Lord Byron stayed to learn Armenian.
Open: daily 15.00 to 17.00 hours.
Vaporetto: route 20.

◆
SAN MICHELE
This is the cemetery island, as can be seen by its sepulchral white walls and the tall, dark cypress trees beyond. The beautiful 15th-century church of **San Michele in Isola** is of interest to students of Renaissance artchitecture, but

the cemetery (accessible from 07.30 to 16.00 hours) is even sadder than could be expected, for dead Venetians cannot rest there long. While the famous – such as the composer Stravinsky, the poet Ezra Pound and the ballet impresario Diaghilev – are allowed to remain, nearly all Venetians buried here are disinterred after a period and their bones scattered on a reef made of their ancestors' remains in a remote reach of the lagoon. The visitor cannot fail to be confronted by evidence that here death, as well as life, is transitory.
Vaporetto: routes 41 and 42.

◆◆◆
TORCELLO ✓

Torcello was the first island to be settled by refugees from the barbarian invasion of the 5th century. At the height of its power, the population was said to have numbered 20,000 but the growth of the more distant and secure Venice, the silting of its creek and the prevalence of malaria reduced it to the level of the other small islands of the lagoon by the 15th century. Now its few score inhabitants grow vines and vegetables and run three notable restaurants. Lying close to the mainland marshes and more than six miles (9.5km) to the northeast of Venice, the little green island offers peace after the bustling city and relaxation in walks along its narrow footpaths. Its great monument is the cathedral of **Santa Maria dell' Assunta**, where the

'Judgement Day' – magnificent mosaics adorn the walls of Santa Maria dell' Assunta on the island of Torcello

extraordinary Byzantine mosaics – notably a tall and compelling *Madonna and Child* and a vast depiction of *Judgement Day* – have been restored.

The whole island, including the cathedral, the small church of **Santa Fosco**, the archaeological museum and the surrounding farmland, is easily explored and can be combined with lunch on a day-trip from Venice without making an early start or expecting a late return. *Vaporetto:* route 14.

59

Mainland

Expeditions to the mainland can be made by train, bus, hired car and even by boat. The hinterland – the Veneto – was long ruled by Venice and so it is marked by Venetian taste both in its towns and in its country villas.

Italy's second oldest university town, Padova makes an ideal expedition to the mainland. Palazzo della Ragione (below) stands between two colourful markets

◆◆◆
PADOVA (PADUA)

The nearest large town to Venice with a population of a quarter of a million, Padova can be reached by train, bus, car – or by boat. The latter, the *Burchiello* and its rival the *Ville del Brenta,* sail between April and October from San Marco at about 09.00 hours (times and fares available from hotel concierges, travel agents and tourist information offices), cross the lagoon and cruise up

the Brenta Canal, which is, in fact, a river. Stopping at several magnificent Renaissance villas on its banks and for lunch at *Il Burchiello* restaurant, they arrive at Padua between 1800 and 1830, and the 23-mile (37km) return journey to Venice is made by bus or train.

A Venetian university city since the 15th century – and rich in buildings of that century – Padova is now dominated by commerce.

◆◆◆
VERONA

Verona lies west of Vicenza (see below) and close to Lake Garda It is most famous as the setting of Shakespeare's play *Romeo and Juliet* and for its Roman remains, notably a magnificent arena, which is sometimes used for performances of opera.

◆◆◆
VICENZA

The capital of the Veneto is Vicenza, a handsome city, for which the great architect Andrea di Palladio – a native of Padova – designed a dozen buildings. With a population of about 120,000, it lies 32 miles (51km) from Venice.

A smaller but equally busy town is **Treviso**, less than 20 miles (32km) from Venice and noted for its good and fashionable restaurants.

Hill-Towns

Northward from the lagoon stand the Alps with Austria beyond.

◆◆◆
ASOLO

The most beautiful of the hinterland towns, Asolo lies in the foothills of the Alps 40 miles (64km) from Venice. A charming town of some 6,000 inhabitants, its old houses – sometimes arcaded at street level as is the custom in hill-towns – cluster around squares and narrow streets and overlook a landscape decorated with villas and cypress trees.

Here also is one of the most celebrated hotels in Italy, the **Villa Cipriani** (tel: 0423 952166), especially famous for its fine cuisine.

For clean mountain air and stunning views, head north and explore the majestic Dolomites

◆◆◆
BASSANO DEL GRAPPA

In the foothills of the Alps, nearly 50 miles (80km) north-west of Venice, this town of 37,000 inhabitants was once under Venetian rule. Formerly renowned for its school of painting, it now produces colourful pottery, which is sold in Venice and throughout northern Italy.

There are some fine old buildings and a famous covered wooden bridge – the **Ponte degli Coperto** – which has been rebuilt several times since the early 13th century. Bassano is noted for the strong alcoholic spirit, *Grappa,* and its restaurants for game and mushrooms from the surrounding hills.

The town is a good centre for exploring the mountains – particularly **Monte Grappa**, which was an Italian stronghold during World War I – and the battlefields Ernest Hemingway described in *A Farewell to Arms.*

Further north and into the Alps is the handsome old town of **Belluno** and beyond it the Dolomite Mountains and the celebrated resort of **Cortina** – renowned for winter sports and summer walking. Austria is also just within range of a day's excursion.

◆
POSSAGNO

Anyone eager to see more works of art should visit the village of Possagno, 45 miles

(72km) northwest of Venice, the home of the sculptor Antonio Canova. Born here in 1757, Canova became the greatest of the neoclassical sculptors, producing smoothly graceful figures and delicate portraits, including his famous busts of Napoleon and Josephine, which are now in galleries throughout the world.

His house is now the centre of a gallery devoted to his works, mostly plaster models for statuary, and in the parish church which he gave to the village – the **Tempio di Canova**, inspired by the Parthenon in Athens and the Pantheon in Rome – is his tomb. However, only his body lies here; his heart remains in Venice, within the pyramid he himself designed for Titian in the great church of the Frari (► 28).

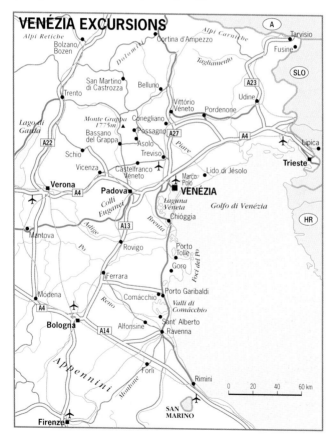

VENÉZIA EXCURSIONS

Going East

◆
LIDO DI JÉSOLO

This seaside resort is along the Adriatic coast to the east of Venice. It has a good beach, caters principally for package holidays, and is reached by bus from Venice.

The Roman Theatre at Trieste, evidence of its ancient beginnings

◆◆
TRIESTE

Further east of Venice than Lido di Jésolo is the great seaport of Trieste, once part of the Austro-Hungarian Empire and now connected with Venice by rail.

A little further to the north, just across the Slovenian border, is **Lipica**, where the Lipizzaner white horses are bred and can be ridden.

PEACE AND QUIET

Countryside and Wildlife in and around Venice

by Paul Sterry

For an island city so completely dominated by buildings, Venice might seem an unpromising destination for the holiday naturalist. Venice and the Veneto coast have considerable wildlife interest and the city makes a good base from which to explore the watery habitat surrounding it. Venice lies in the Laguna Veneta, a marine lagoon near the mouth of the River Po which is almost completely cut off from the sea by sand bars. The lagoon is studded with islands and saltmarsh, the whole area being a haven for wildlife, in particular birds. Ducks, waders, egrets and herons are all numerous at certain times of the year. Although much of the Po delta and Laguna Veneta are inaccessible, many species can be seen during boat trips or from the adjacent mainland. By way of a complete contrast, those who want a few days' break from Venice can make a comparatively short journey north through sunny hillsides to the Italian Alps.

Venice and the Venetian Lagoon

Visitors to Venice might be forgiven for supposing that, after people, pigeons and cats are not just the commonest residents of the city but its *only* living inhabitants. However true this might seem at first glance, a more thorough tour

of even the city itself will turn up a surprising number of birds, and a boat tour to one of the other islands is sure to enthral.

Parks and gardens, however small, in the quieter backstreets of Venice are likely to host serins. These delightful little relatives of the canary sing a beautiful, twittering song throughout spring and early summer, usually from the topmost branches of a tree. Search the lower branches and dense foliage of bushes and you may find a variety of warblers; melodious warblers, blackcaps, lesser whitethroats and even Sardinian warblers can all be seen. Although the spring migration period is the best time of year for seeing these birds, some of them linger on into the summer months.

Black redstarts are also found in parks and gardens but are equally at home on the roofs of houses. Some individuals can become quite confiding and seem not to be bothered at all by people. Gulls frequent the shores of the lagoon and sometimes congregate where boats and larger ships are moored. The yellow-legged race of herring gull is most often seen in the winter months but black-headed gulls are frequent all year round. Scrutinise each one carefully because the somewhat similar Mediterranean gull is also often numerous. In its summer plumage, this is one of the most elegant of gulls and sports a black hood, red eye-

Black redstarts are equally at home in the countryside or the city

ring and pure white wings. It has a distinctive 'cow-cow' call. Boat trips between the islands in the Laguna Veneta pass the occasional undisturbed shoreline and areas of reedbed. Waders, grey herons and little egrets, the latter species easily recognised by its white plumage, black legs and bright yellow feet, prefer the open shores. Marsh harriers, reed warblers, buntings and purple herons, on the other hand, favour the sanctuary provided by the reeds. Unfortunately, boat trips generally offer only fleeting glimpses of these habitats and to study them in more detail it is probably best to return to mainland Italy and explore the Po delta from there.

The Po Delta, Valli di Comacchio and Punte Alberte

To the south of Venice and the Laguna Veneta lies the delta of the River Po, which drains into the Gulf of Venice. At one time, the wetland areas along the coast would have been continuous and would have comprised vast areas of brackish lagoons and saltmarsh. However, centuries of exploitation have affected many of the more accessible areas of the River Po's valley and delta and reduced its value to wildlife: commercial development and changed land use of landward regions have encouraged the growth of towns and vast acreages of rice fields and other agricultural land.

Despite man's influence on the valley of the River Po, considerable areas of the delta's coastal fringe still remain largely untouched. Some are protected by their inaccessibility, others by reserve status as with the Riserva Naturale Bocche di Po, north of Ravenna. These wetlands are a haven for breeding, migrant and wintering birds and, despite the inevitable difficulties in viewing such a water-bound region, boat tours from Porto Tolle or Goro and coastal roads afford tantalising but exciting glimpses of the wildlife.

Spring in the Po delta sees the arrival of thousands of migrant birds from their wintering grounds in Africa. Black terns, with smaller numbers of whiskered terns and white-winged black terns, are sometimes seen in small flocks catching insects over open water. Their larger relatives, Caspian terns and common terns, dive for fish and crustaceans and are occasionally seen with the smallest member of the gull family in Europe, the little gull. Shallow water around lagoon margins and at the edges of islands, attracts a wide variety of wading birds, which feed mainly on small invertebrates and fish. Most elegant of these is the black-winged stilt, whose long, red legs allow it to feed in deeper water than its equally distinctive relative, the avocet. This latter species has black and white plumage and a thin, upturned bill which is scythed through the water. Ruff, redshanks, marsh sandpipers, dunlin and Temminck's stints also pass through in spring and

many stop off on autumn migration as well to feed and rest. Although each species has its own preferred habitat, mixed flocks are often seen, testing the identification skills of most birdwatchers.

The Valli di Comacchio is a large brackish lagoon situated between the mouth of the River Po and Ravenna to the south. Almost all the species found in the Po delta also occur here, but access to this enormous area is effectively restricted to viewing from the road between Porto Garibaldi on the coast and Comacchio, or the road which runs along the west side of the lagoon from Comacchio south to Alfonsine.

The stately great egret is an

The elegant grey heron can be spotted off the more remote islands

occasional winter visitor to the Valli di Comacchio, but more frequent in the summer months is its smaller relative, the little egret. Undisturbed breeding habitat for this bird, and many other species of heron, has been drastically reduced over the years but at the Oasi di Protezione di Punte Alberte (Wildlife Oasis of Punte Alberte), healthy populations of egrets, herons and ducks can be found. Situated between the Valli di Comacchio and Ravenna, and managed by the Italian branch of the World Wide Fund for Nature, Punte Alberte can be viewed by the public from its perimeter. For access to the reserve itself and its observation tower, contact the WWF for further information.

The Po Valley

The low-lying land that forms the valley of the River Po dominates the whole of northern Italy and stretches from Turin in the west to the Venetian coast in the east. This huge area with its fertile soils is, understandably, subject to intensive cultivation, but this is not always to the detriment of wildlife. Flooded fields support large numbers of water birds, while if you look carefully you will find that marshes, wet meadows, lakes and even drainage ditches harbour colourful plants, fish and amphibians.

The rice fields, which are such a feature of much of the Po valley, offer rich feeding for birds. Grey herons, purple herons, night herons and little egrets as well as black-winged stilts and other migrant waders can be found in most areas. However, their abundance and exact distribution is dependent upon the time of year and the precise environmental conditions: seasonal planting or harvesting may cause the birds to move to new areas. In winter, wildfowl, lapwings and snipe arrive in large numbers from northern Europe and boost the numbers of resident species. Drainage ditches and stream margins soon become overgrown with reeds and other emergent vegetation and are a sanctuary for wildlife. The colourful caterpillars of swallowtail butterflies feed on

Watch out for the bright green tree frog among the vegetation

Little bitterns are more difficult to find, living among the reeds at the water's edge

the leaves of umbellifers. Tree frogs clamber through the vegetation while agile frogs remain in the safety of the waters below. Marsh warblers, crakes and little bitterns are secretive residents, while great reed warblers often announce their presence by singing from a prominent perch. Patches of woodland are the haunt of golden orioles and nightingales, and also attract passage migrant species in spring and autumn. Penduline tits also like woodland borders and build their curious, flask-shaped nests suspended from the end of an overhanging branch.

Agriculture has fortunately left some areas comparatively untouched. Water meadows, although an increasingly rare sight, are home to colourful butterflies and may host flowers such as marsh orchids, Jersey orchids, gladioli and many more.

Open Country
The journey north from Venice leads eventually to the foothills of the Italian Alps, but before this mountainous region is reached, the visitor will find attractive, rolling countryside. Still feeling the influence of the Mediterranean climate, the land enjoys hot summers and mild winters and is consequently

The distinctive markings of the swallowtail larva on milk parsley

dotted with olive groves and vineyards. In spring, colourful flowers and butterflies abound and birds find a haven here as well. Tilled soils untouched by herbicides become a riot of colour in spring: poppies, corn marigolds, asphodels, bugloss, grape hyacinths, star thistles and gladioli can all be abundant under the right conditions. Although the heat of summer withers the vegetation to a uniform brown, the few weeks in spring when plants are in flower more than make up for the months of desiccation. Of course, wildflowers are colourful and fragrant not for our benefit, but to attract insects which serve as pollinating agents. Chafer beetles, hummingbird hawk moths and butterflies such as swallowtails, scarce swallowtails, dappled white, black-veined white and green

hairstreak are frequent visitors, some falling victim to praying mantids or crab spiders.

The bare soils of vineyards are favoured feeding grounds for birds such as crested lark, short-toed lark, tawny pipit and that most typically Mediterranean bird, the hoopoe. These can be difficult to spot since they feed unobtrusively on the ground, but easier to find are woodchat shrikes, lesser grey shrikes and red-backed shrikes. Although these attractively marked species are songbirds, they behave like miniature birds of prey, perching on wires and posts and swooping down on unsuspecting prey such as beetles and grasshoppers. They also have the rather macabre habit of impaling their larger catches so that they can be more easily torn up.

Black-eared wheatears and

corn buntings are also found in this rolling countryside. The jingling song of the latter species is a familiar sound as is the twittering song of the serin. Unmistakeable and truly evocative of the Mediterannean, however, is the bubbling call of the bee-eater. As its name suggests, the bee-eater does indeed catch insects, and parties of these extraodinarily colourful birds are often seen gliding and swooping over vineyards, orchards and olive groves.

The Italian Alps
Popular both with residents of the Venetian coast and visitors to Veneto, the Italian Alps are a frequent weekend destination during the winter skiing season. In addition to the attraction of winter sports, the Alps offer spectacular scenery and wildlife to match this grandeur. Although winter is the 'high' season, a visit during the summer can be equally worth while; plants and animals abound and temperatures are warm and pleasant. This can make a refreshing change from Venice where the heat during July and August can be oppressive.
Despite increasing public pressure, the Alps remain Italy's last wilderness region. Cloaked in forests of beech, hazel and Scots pine at lower elevations, arolla pines, white firs and larches grow to the tree line at about 6,000 feet (1,800m). Above this, scree slopes and colourful alpine meadows cover the landscape,

restricted only by the line of permanent snow fields and glaciers which blanket the highest peaks.
Although almost any area of the Alps is worth exploring, a few areas in particular deserve a special mention. The **Foresta Tarvisio** (Tarvisio Forest) and adjacent **Parco Naturale di Fusine** (Fusine Natural Park), close to the Slovenian and Austrian borders in the Julian Alps, have forests, high mountains and beautiful lakes. The **Riservas Naturale Val Tovanella, Schiara Occid** and **Monti del Sole** and the **Parco Naturale Panveggio-Pale di San Martino** near Belluno are also stunningly attractive and are especially good for flowers, while the **Parco Naturale Adamello-Brenta** near Trento may still support a small population of European brown bears, now sadly on the verge of extinction.
From May until July, alpine meadows are colourful with flowers such as spring gentian, trumpet gentian, alpine snowbell, edelweiss, bird's-eye primrose and globeflower, and are the haunt of alpine marmots, alpine choughs, snow finches and chamois. Water pipits, rock thrushes, ptarmigan and alpine accentors favour the scree and boulder slopes, while golden eagles and the occasional griffon vulture circle overhead on the lookout for carrion. At least part of the eagle's diet is also live prey, which may include high altitude species, such as alpine hares and young chamois.

The wooded lower slopes provide sanctuary for red deer, roe deer, red squirrels and a wide variety of forest birds. Citril finches usually nest near the tree line while lower down, Bonelli's warblers, crested tits, treecreepers, nutcrackers and hazelhens can be found, the latter, however, only by luck and persistent searching. Several species of woodpecker also occur in the Italian Alps, including white-backed and three-toed woodpeckers, as well as the largest European species, the black woodpecker. Spring is the best season for seeing woodpeckers as well as most other woodland birds, because at this time of year they are displaying or singing at the start of the breeding season. Glades and forest rides are good places to look for woodland flowers in spring and summer. Bellflowers, spiked rampion, purple coltsfoot and several species of orchids occur, including the attractive but distinctly local lady's slipper orchid. It goes without saying that none of these species should be picked.

Birds-eye primrose; just one of the bright flowers of summer

FOOD AND DRINK

Its reputation for dull, unimaginative cooking, high prices and surly service is not fair to Venice. It is true that restaurants tend to be more expensive than those on the mainland, since almost everything but some of the fish has to be imported by barge; and along the tourist trails the waiters can become as jaded as their customers, particularly in summer.

That said, the visitor can eat well in Venice. Those enjoying the higher *trattoria* style of cooking will not be disappointed. Venetian restaurants offer the same range of basic Italian dishes as will be found throughout the country but their local specialities are more simple than those of, say, Florence, Bologna or Rome. For a first course try fish soup – *zuppa di pesce* – which is so full of shellfish, shrimps and white fish that it is best followed by something light; or Parma ham – *prosciutto crudo* – with fresh figs.

Two of the most familiar Venetian main dishes are acquired tastes: sliced calves' liver with onion (*fegato alla Veneziana*) and squid (*seppie*) cooked in its own black ink with cornmeal cake (*polenta*). Venetians are good at creating delectable sweets, particularly the light and creamy *tiramisú*, a delicious cold confection of chocolate, coffee, marscapone cheese and brandy.

Another way to get a taste of Italian food is to try some of the many local snacks (*cichetti*) available, usually displayed on counters. These include garlicky meatballs (*polpette*), mini-pizzas (*pizzetas*), various types of seafood and slices of fried vegetables.

When ordering drinks, '*una ombra*' (which means 'shade') will produce a glass of white house wine, unless you request *rosso* (red). *Ombra* comes from the old tradition of drinking wine in the shade of the Piazza. For a detailed description of Venetian food, plus recipes, read *The Food of Italy Region by Region* by Claudia Roden (published by Vintage).

Restaurants

Restaurants in the middle and upper-middle range are generally cheaper than their equivalents in Britain and waiters are more often friendly than not. Many restaurants display a set-price *menu turistico* offering a choice of three or four dishes (*piatti*) for each course; this can be an inexpensive way of tasting a number of Venetian specialities. There are some 300 restaurants in the city. Some close in the low seasons and many shut on Sundays and Mondays, except those in hotels and the grander of these serve food suitable to their style, often out of doors in summer. Particularly recommended are the restaurants in the **Gritti Palace,** the **Danieli**, the **Monaco e Grand Canal** and the **Londra Palace** (► Hotels, 86–8).

The Cipriani Restaurants

Venetian restaurants owe much to the Cipriani family, who have given them a smart yet friendly style. The hotel named after them is now owned by Sea Containers, which also runs the Orient Express, but the family still run three notable restaurants which deserve pride of place, although they do now tend to be more expensive and attract the 'in-crowd'.

Harry's Bar, Calle Vallaresso, San Marco 1323 (tel: 041 528577).

This was the original Cipriani establishment, a favourite haunt of Ernest Hemingway, who would eat and drink in the downstairs bar, which is more amusing than the grander restaurant upstairs. It still has an air of the 1930s as do many of its customers – the richer expatriate residents of the city and the more eccentric and affluent Venetians – and there is often so much to watch indoors that nobody tries to look at the view through the opaque windows. The food is delicious and quite expensive, although it is difficult to improve on a very simple meal of their speciality, *tagliolini verdi gratinati* (green pasta with chopped ham in a cheese sauce) and a jug of chilled Soave white wine from the Veneto.

Harry's Dolci, Fondamento San Biagio, Giudecca 773 (tel: 041 5224844).

Over on Giudecca island, the same management have opened a restaurant – originally designed as a tea-room – next to their own bakery. This serves much the same sort of food as Harry's

Bar, but with emphasis on sweets and cakes, as the word *dolci* implies. In summer, tables are set beside the water to command the view of passing ships and the Zattere waterfront beyond.

Locanda Cipriani, Piazza Santa Fosca 29, Torcello (tel: 041 730150)

The third and most delectable endowment by this family is on the island of Torcello to the northeast of Venice itself. It is open from Wednesday to Sunday between mid-March and October. Another favourite of Hemingway's, this looks like a country inn from the outside but is a smart restaurant within. Its particular joy is lunch outside among the flowers and vegetables of the walled garden with the tower of the cathedral just beyond. Again the food is Cipriani-style and fairly expensive but in fine, warm weather a meal here – combined with a visit to the cathedral and the voyage from Venice and back – can be a high-point of a holiday.

Eating by the Water

Waterside meals are a particular Venetian pleasure and these can be enjoyed on the Zattere or by quiet canals. There is a row of relatively cheap and cheerful *pizzerie* lining the *fondamenta* at this end of the Zattere, with tables on wooden platforms built out over the water. Here, beside the bridge over the San Trovaso canal, pizza with wine followed by ice-cream and coffee provides an excuse for sitting

Spend a lazy lunch by the waterside

an hour or so in the sun, and is not expensive.

La Cuisina, Calle Larga XXII Marzo, San Marco 2161 (tel: 041 5213785)

This luxury restaurant must surely be one of the city's most romantic, with its terrace on the Grand Canal overlooking the Salute church and the island of San Giorgio. Booking essential.

Hosteria da Franz, Fondamenta San Giuseppe, Castello 754 (tel: 041 5220861)

This restaurant, with its picturesque canalside terrace,

serves some of the best
seafood in Venice. Booking
recommended.
Riviera, Zattere, Dorsoduro
1473 (tel: 041 5227621).
This restaurant has been
opened in a former religious
building (on the façade stands a
statue of a saint with a pig
beside him; he is the patron
saint of sausage-makers). In
fine weather, tables are set
outside by the water and the
delicious food is slightly
cheaper than at Cipriani
restaurants.

Garden Restaurants
Gardens are much more
unusual than water in Venice,
so restaurants with the former
rightly make much of eating
beneath a vine in a sun-
dappled courtyard, or under
Venetian lanterns at night.
Da Ignazio, Calle dei Saoneria,
San Polo 2, 749 (tel: 041
5234852).
On the same side of the Canal
Grande as the Trattoria Nono
Risorto (see below), this is a
courtyard restaurant.
Montin, Fondamenta di Borgo,
Dorsoduro 1147 (tel: 041
5227151).
Among the best-known garden
restaurants, it has a large
garden and is cheerful and
cosy inside when too cold for
eating outdoors. It is difficult to
find in a quiet and charming
district near the Campo San
Barnaba, but so popular that
booking is usually essential.
Trattoria Nono Risorto, Calle
della Regina, Santa Croce 2331
(tel: 041 5241169).
Close to the Rialto markets, this
is another restaurant with a

large garden, which also
displays the work of
contemporary artists. Like
Montin, this specialises in
simple Venetian dishes such as
spaghetti with shellfish, mixed
fried fish, squid with *polenta*
and liver *Veneziana*.

Others
As an alternative to looking at
water or boats, the passing
throng is also a Venetian
pleasure and some restaurants
have tables out in a *campo*.
Amongst many cheerful,
unpretentious and typically
Venetian *trattorie* is **Al
Bacareto**, San Marco 3447 (tel:
041 5289336), close to Campo
Santo Stefano.
Ai Corazzieri, Salizzada dei
Corazzieri, Castello 3839 (tel:
041 5289859). This small but
charming restaurant is hidden
away behind the Campo
Bandiera e Moro and the La
Residenza hotel (► **Hotels**, 86).
Here one of the most delicious
Venetian dishes is *tagliolini con
cappe sante*: pasta with 'saints'
heads', small scallops in
piquant sauce.
Ai Gondolieri, Campo San Vio,
Dorsoduro 366 (tel: 041
5286396). Housed in an old
inn, this restaurant specialises
in Venetian cooking. It is
situated between the
Accademia bridge and the
Collezione Guggenheim (►
Museums, 46).

Each district has its own little
restaurants and there will
always be several near each
bed-and-breakfast hotel.
Tourist menus with dishes at
less than the à la carte prices
are usually satisfactory but are

unlikely to include the more interesting specialities. In restaurants of any class it is permissible to order pasta as a main course, so reducing the cost of the meal.

It can generally be assumed that the bill will include a

Valpolicella, one of the best red wines from the Veneto, is a perfect accompaniment to local dishes

service charge (ask if uncertain) but Venetians do generally add an extra 1,000 *lire* a head as a further tip for the waiter.

Cafés, Bars and Snack Bars

Cafés have long played an important part in Venetian life, particularly in the exchange of news and gossip. In the Piazza San Marco 56–9, **Florian** (tel:

A drink in Piazza S Marco is expensive – so, like the atmosphere, make it an experience to savour

041 5285338), which opened in 1720, was a centre of political dissent during Austrian rule in the 19th century, while the Austrians patronised **Quadri**, Piazza San Marco 120-4 (tel: 041 5222105), on the opposite side of the square and their orchestras still compete for attention. Both are expensive and the cost of a cup of coffee at either should be regarded as the price of an experience of street theatre. In cold weather, the interior of Florian – all faded plush and 19th-century murals – is redolent of the last century.

> At any café, bar or snack bar, a seat at a table usually doubles the bill but many of the smaller establishments serve only at the bar and lack even chairs.

All the major hotels have bars, of course, but the most celebrated in the city is **Harry's Bar**, Calle Vallaresso, San Marco 1323 (tel: 041 528577), near the San Marco *vaporetto* pier (► 74). The speciality is the Bellini – peach juice and champagne – and the house wines are excellent. It also serves the most succulent (and expensive) sandwiches; indeed these are usually good, and with generous fillings, in many Venetian bars.

SHOPPING

Venice has always been a city for shopping. Over the centuries its merchants made the city's fortune by selling wholesale the merchandise of the East to fellow-Europeans; now its hundreds of enticing little shops sell Venetian arts and crafts and the produce of Italy to visitors.

There are no noteworthy department stores in Venice so shopping should be combined with sightseeing throughout the city. The most fashionable shopping areas are in and to the north and west of the Piazza San Marco and on and around the Rialto bridge; the busiest, along the wide Strada Nuovo leading from the railway station into the heart of the city. All over Venice attractive little shops can be found, sometimes combined with workshops making the goods on sale. While the windows of clothes shops and shoe shops will catch the eye with their displays of the latest fashions from Rome and Milan, visitors may want to take home something that is peculiarly Venetian. Some ideas may be found in the sections below. Most shops accept the major credit cards and will pack and mail or freight purchases to their final destination.

Fabrics

As can be seen in the paintings of Venetian life in past centuries, richly coloured and textured fabrics were always favoured. They still are and a new process of printing part-rayon fabric with traditional

Venetian designs has produced a new range suitable for curtains, loose covers, cushion-covers and bedspreads. **Bevilacqua**, Ponte della Canonica, San Marco 337 (tel: 041 5287581) has an exquisite selection of both machine- and hand-woven fabrics, some made on original 17th-century looms. Some of the patterns at **Gaggio**, Calle delle Botteghe, San Marco 3451, near the Campo San Stefano (Tel: 041 522 8574) are those once favoured by the designer and artist Mariano Fortuny (1871–1949), best remembered for the light, pleated silk dresses he produced. His fabric designs are the speciality of **Trois**, Campo San Maurizio, San Marco 2666 (tel: 041 5222905). Lace is made and sold by the women of the island of Burano beyond Murano.

Glass

Surprisingly, the Venetians, who have always had such good taste in art and architecture, have turned out a remarkable amount of vulgar nick-nacks during their millennium of glass-making. Today the bulk of the glass on display in shop windows and showrooms is over-ornate, ostentatious and impractical; vast ornaments, dinky souvenirs and wineglasses that are difficult to use and easy to break. That said, it is worth searching for the beautiful pieces that are still made with a purity of design and strong Venetian character.

For eight centuries, Murano has been the glass-making island. Glass shops and showrooms abound in the city itself but when a visitor is invited to watch glass-blowing there, it will only be a demonstration in a back room: for the real thing, Murano must be visited and there, too, are the most comprehensive showrooms. Take time in choosing glass and do not be deflected by sales-talk which has been polished over the centuries. After a purchase, retailers and manufacturers are efficient at packing and freighting it.

For most people, the more strongly made and well-designed jugs, wineglasses and vases are the best buys. Children love the little glass animals, figures and trinkets that are often made in the glass shops themselves.

On Murano – reached by *vaporetto* from the Fondamenta Nuove, or by a *circolare* ferry from elsewhere in the city – the leading manufacturers are **Barovier e Toso**, Fondamenta Vetrai 28, Murano (tel: 041 739049), and elegant table glass can be bought from **Mazzega**, Fondamenta da Mula 147, Murano (tel: 041 736888) and **Ars Cenedese Murano**, Fondamenta Venier 48, Murano (tel: 041 739101). The most comprehensive showroom on the island is **CAM** in the Piazzale Colonna (tel: 041 739944).

In the city itself the best-known glass shops are in and around the Piazza San Marco and a particularly wide selection is displayed by **Battison**, Calle Vallaresso, San Marco 1320

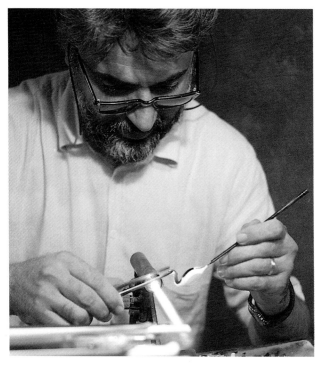

The master of glass ornaments, Amadi; at work on a delicate glass bird

(tel: 041 5230509), near the San Marco *vaporetto* pier. An expedition to the far side of the Canal Grande will find the finest maker of glass ornaments – exquisite birds, insects and fruit – made in the little shop, **Amadi**, Calle Saoneri, San Polo 2747 (tel: 041 5238089).

Glass costume jewellery is often cheap and attractive and antique Venetian glass beads are sometimes made up as earrings and brooches, as at the **Beads Shop**, Calle San Provolo, Castello 4719 (tel: 041 5286946).

Leather

Fine leatherwork is, of course, an Italian speciality and there are many smart shops selling handbags, briefcases, belts and shoes throughout the city. One particularly elegant shop is **Vogini**, Calle Ascensione, San Marco 1257 – 1301 (tel: 041 5222573), close to the San Marco *vaporetto* pier. For supremely elegant and expensive shoes, look at the window displays in the main designer stores along Calle

Vallaresso, Salizada San Moisè and Calle Goldoni. To see a typical shop and workshop combined, visit **Cose di Pelle**, Campo Santa Margherita, Dorsoduro 2946.

Metalwork

Small foundries and smithies still abound in the alleys of Venice, notably to the north of the Campo San Barnaba. They not only manufacture brass

Masks for the carnival or to give as presents – Tragicomica has hundreds

souvenirs – such as Lion of St Mark paperweights – but make practical and attractive coat-hooks, door-knockers and so on. Some of the old-established workshops also stock antique metalwork, which is not expensive. One such is **Rossetin Sergio**, Ca'Foscari, Dorsoduro (tel: 041 5224195). There are many silver shops and some silversmiths throughout the city. Most of their stock is manufactured elsewhere – such as the charming little silver boxes fashioned like sea shells – but a

few both manufacture and sell, amongst them **Sfriso**, Campo San Toma, San Polo 2849 (tel: 041 5223558).

Paper

The fashion for marbled Italian paper applied to book covers, picture frames, stationery holders, blotters, pencils, ornaments and so on has taken hold of Venice and such shops often sell beautifully coloured silk scarves and ties as well. A particularly elegant stock of hand-printed paper and silk is offered by **Alberto Valese-Ebru** at three shops, Salizzada San Samuele, San Marco 3135 (tel: 041 5200921), Calle della Fenice, San Marco 1920 (tel: 041 5286302) and Campiello Santo Stefano 3471. Another with a particularly wide range of paper is **Legatoria Piazzesi**, Campiello della Fettrina, San Marco 2511 (tel: 041 5221205). During the decade since the revival of the winter carnival, mask-shops and mask-makers have proliferated. Many of those produced are over-elaborate and have lost the charm and sophistication of masks made when the fashion was first revived. However, unpainted, white *papier-mâché* masks, which can be painted by the purchaser, are offered by **Ca'Macana**, Calle delle Botteghe, Dorsoduro 3172, close to the Ca'Rezzonico (tel: 041 5203229), and masks can be seen being decorated at **La Mano,** Calle Longa, Castello 5175 (tel: 041 529995). Masks and costumes for the carnival can be bought from **Tragicomica,** Calle dei Nomboli, San Polo 2800 (tel: 041 721102), and at **Balo Coloc**, Calle Lunga, Santa Croce 2134 (tel: 041 5240551), which also stocks a remarkable range of hats.

Woodwork

Venetian craftsmen have produced painted and gilded furniture and frames for centuries, usually to charming baroque designs, and they still do. Furniture can be expensive and generally has to be freighted to its destination but frames for pictures and mirrors are often cheap, charming and more portable. Shops and workshops are scattered throughout the city but there are a number in the alleys to the immediate north and east of the Campo San Barnaba, one such being **Manuela Canestrelli,** San Barnaba, Dorsoduro 2779 (tel: 041 5230602). Another in the Campo San Stefano on the far side of the Accademia bridge is **Gianni Cavalier**, San Marco 2863A (tel: 041 5238621).

Other shoppers are also catered for.

Books

Books about Venice in English are an important part of the stock at **Libreria Internazionale Sangiorgio,** Calle Larga XXII Marzo, San Marco 2087 (tel: 041 5238451). Well-stocked shops for books on Venice and Venetian architecture include **Libreria Sansovino**, Bacino Orseolo 84, Piazza di San Marco (tel: 041 5222623).

Fashion

There are so many smart clothes shops in Venice that the fashion-conscious can spend a day window-shopping instead of looking at Old Master paintings. The well-known **Emporio Armani**, Calle dei Fabbri, San Marco 989, is a good place to start the exploration. In the unlikely event of disappointment, visitors have been known to find exactly what they want in a smart boutique in the departure lounge at Marco Polo Airport on their way home: this **Boutique di Vittorio Testi** is particularly good for men's ties.

Fresh fish from the lagoon is a speciality of some restaurants

Food and Wine

The principal food markets are at the western (San Polo) end of the Rialto Bridge, where fruit and vegetables are sold every morning except Sunday and fish daily except Sunday and Monday. Most of the fish is imported frozen but some – often live – is direct from the lagoon and the Adriatic. Near by are several small shops selling a variety of cheese. Other fruit, vegetable and fish stalls are often to be found in the Strada Nuova (leading into the city from the railway station), in several *campi* – including Campo Santa Margherita – and there is a barge selling fruit and vegetables moored in the canal alongside the Campo San Barnaba. Grocers' shops, butchers and bakers are scattered throughout the city. The wines of the Veneto – and those from further afield – are sold in grocers' shops throughout the city.

Markets

Stalls selling silk scarves and ties and leather goods are set up at either end of the Rialto Bridge, upon which are two parallel rows of little shops selling jewellery, leather goods, silks and shoes. Stalls are also found in the Strada Nuova and those selling souvenirs congregate along the Riva degli Schiavoni; these include artists mass-producing views of Venice and offering instant caricatures. About twice a year an antiques market is held in the Campo San Maurizio.

ACCOMMODATION

There are about 200 hotels in Venice and, this being Italy, most of them are well run. A few may have become slatternly through over-confidence induced by a non-stop flow of package tourists, but their principal handicap is age. A medieval palace, religious institution or merchant's house cannot be converted into a modern hotel with identical bedrooms, although ruthless use of steel joists has opened up many a spacious lobby behind a Renaissance façade. Thus the same hotel is likely to offer both large and lofty bedrooms commanding magnificent views and dark poky rooms overlooking a dank ventilation well or an alley. If a particular hotel is known to command fine views, suitable rooms can usually be reserved at an extra charge. Lone travellers are particularly at risk since single rooms are the most cramped. One solution for those accustomed to travelling alone and staying in the more expensive hotels is to choose one that is less expensive and book a double room.

Venice is a remarkably quiet city but for light sleepers there is the hazard of church bells in the early morning and the hooters and bellowing diesels of barges on the wider canals. For most visitors the chance of such disturbance is an acceptable risk.

Now that the city is busy at Christmas and Easter and the February carnival has been

Near the Palazzo Ducale, the Danieli is Venice's largest hotel, boasting such visitors as Dickens and Wagner

reintroduced, there are fewer times of year when it can seem empty. These currently are November, the first three weeks of December, January and March, when some hotels may close. The busiest months are July, August and September.

Most Venetian hotels now serve only breakfast and only the grandest offer a cooked breakfast. A number have good restaurants but, as a general rule, half-board should be avoided because this nearly always involves the evening meal and so hampers the enjoyable exploration of the city's restaurants (▶ 73–9). The tourist information offices at Piazzale Roma (in the Autorimessa Communale garage); on the Tronchetto; at Santa Lucia railway station; Marco Polo airport; and the Venice exit of the autostrada at Marghera all operate a hotel booking service. If a room is found the 10,000 *lire* deposit is deducted from your first night's bill.

Expensive Hotels
There are a dozen very grand hotels in Venice, most of them, suitably, on the Grand Canal near San Marco.

Bauer Grünwald e Grand Hotel, Campo San Moisè, San Marco 1459 (tel: 041 5207022). The land-side of this hotel is modern but its canal façade reveals that it was once a splendid palazzo. Today it has an opulence designed for the plutocracy. It offers views over the Grand Canal.

Bonvecchiati, Calle Goldoni, San Marco 4488 (tel: 041 5285017). Situated close to the Piazza San Marco, this is one of the more expensive hotels which cater for package holidays.
Although it lacks the distinctive Venetian character, it is comfortable and well placed for exploring the city.

Cipriani, Giudecca 10 (tel: 041 5207744). Across the water on the otherwise unfashionable island of Giudecca is the Cipriani, the caravanserai of the rich and smart. Elegant and

comfortable as the former religious institution buildings now are, they lack the character of Venice itself, which lies across the Basin of San Marco and is reached in five minutes by the hotel's free ferry. Its principal asset is its magnificent open-air swimming pool, a miraculous cure for fatigue after a long day's sightseeing in the city. Non-residents lunching at the hotel may be allowed to use the pool if it is not crowded, but the charge is expensive.

Danieli, Riva degli Schiavoni, Castello 4196 (tel: 041 5226480). Another new hotel building is the bleak modern wing of the Danieli, almost next to the Doges' Palace and overlooking the Basin of San Marco, which makes this hotel the largest in Venice. Guests have included some of the city's most famous visitors – Dickens, Wagner and Proust among them – and the original building has atmosphere and style in its public rooms but is not above catering to the upper end of the package holiday market.

Gabrielli Sandwirth, Riva degli Schiavoni, Castello 4110 (tel: 041 5231580). This is a former Gothic *palazzo* with its architectural splendours incorporated into its public rooms, courtyard and rose garden; but here, too, single rooms can be cell-sized.

Gritti Palace, Santa Maria del Giglio, San Marco 2467 (tel: 041 794611). This must be the queen of all the Venetian grand hotels. It was built as a *palazzo*

Not only the queen of Venetian hotels, but one of the best in Europe – the Gritti Palace stands on the Grand Canal

in the 15th century and sumptuously coverted. In summer, its principal delight is the open-air **Terrazza del Doge**, where meals are served beside the Grand Canal. It also rents out furnished apartments for a minimum of one week.

Londra Palace, Riva degli Schiavoni, Castello 4171 (tel: 041 5200533). This is one of the hotels along the Riva degli Schiavoni – so overlooking the Basin of San Marco. It is efficiently run and comfortable.

Luna, Calle dell' Ascensione, San Marco 1243 (tel: 041 5289840). Like the Bonvecchiati, this is a comfortable package holiday hotel in the higher price bracket. Its position near the Piazza San Marco is convenient for exploring the city.

Metropole, Riva degli Schiavoni, Castello 4199 (tel: 041 5205044). Another hotel on the Riva degli Schiavoni with a view of the San Marco basin. Comfortable and well run.

Monaco e Grand Canal, Calle Vallaresso, San Marco 1325 (tel: 041 5200211). Many regular visitors to the grander Venetian hotels now recommend the Monaco e Grand Canal, run by a graduate of Harry's Bar, the famous establishment opposite (➤ 74). Like the nearby Gritti Palace, it has tables on a terrace beside the Canal

The S Cassiano is another converted palazzo – where you can arrive in style at its own watergate

Grande and it is only a few steps from the San Marco vaporetto pier. Quiet and cosy, it is also smart and close to the most fashionable shops and the banks.

Moderately Priced Hotels
The following are popular with regular visitors to Venice.

Accademia (tel: 041 5237846). This is a 17th-century house in its own garden at the junction of two canals, just off the Canal Grande. Only breakfast is served (in the garden when warm). Although the hotel is no longer family owned, the management has improved. Its position remains idyllic, particularly when the wisteria is in bloom, and it is convenient for districts away from the tourist trails. It is prudent to ask for a room overlooking the front or back garden as those above the

canal at one side can be noisy with barges in the early morning.

Flora, Calle Bergamaschi, San Marco 2283/A (tel: 041 5205844). Some visitors choose the Flora, largely because of its lush, secluded garden and because it is conveniently close to fashionable shops. Some single rooms are rather bleak and cramped.

La Fenice et Des Artistes, Campiello Fenice, San Marco 1936 (tel: 041 5232333). This hotel is quiet, charmingly furnished and close to the Fenice Theatre.

San Cassiano-Ca' Favretto, Calle della Rosa, Santa Croce 2232 (tel: 041 721033). Some former patrons of the Accademia have transferred their loyalty to the charming San Cassiano, a 14th-century *palazzo* converted into a hotel a few years ago. On the opposite side of the Grand Canal from the glorious Ca' d'Oro palace, it has its own watergate at which guests can be landed, which is an easier way to arrive than through the maze of alleys ashore. The rooms are comfortable and the staff charming but the stairs are steep (there is no lift), so there are two bedrooms on the ground floor especially for those who cannot manage the ascent.

Seguso, Zattere, Dorsoduro 779 (tel: 041 5222340). This long-established, family-run

hotel is situated on the Zattere, facing across the shipping channel to Giudecca island.

Part of the enjoyment of repeated visits to Venice is in trying different hotels and among those recommended for atmosphere and situation as much as efficiency and convenience are these half-dozen:

Ateneo, San Fantin, San Marco 1876 (tel: 041 5200588). This quiet hotel, tucked away in a hidden alley, is near the Fenice Theatre, the smart shops and pleasant *campi.*

Bel Sito e Berlino, Santa Maria del Giglio, San Marco 2517 (tel: 041 5223365). Those wishing to be in the social mainstream but who cannot afford the Gritti Palace choose the Bel Sito, just a short step away and opposite a peculiarly Venetian church with a façade carved with battle rather than Biblical scenes.

Carpaccio, Calle Corner, San Polo 2765 (tel: 041 523553). On the Grand Canal itself, reached by what is claimed to be the narrowest alley in the city, is the Carpaccio, its long *salone* commanding a wonderful view of water and palaces.

La Residenza, Campo Bandiera e Moro, Castello 3608 (tel: 041 5285315). This is another palace where the Gritti family lived, hidden away in a *campo* off the Riva degli Schiavoni. This intensely Venetian *pensione* has a

La Residenza offers atmosphere at a reasonable price

magnificent *salone* on the *piano nobile* with paintings, plasterwork and chandeliers, off which passages lead to comfortable bedrooms. The service is efficient but the management speaks French rather than English to guests.

Pausania, San Barnaba, Dorsoduro 2824 (tel: 041 5222083). This hotel is on a quiet canal where vegetables are sold to housewives direct from a moored barge. It has recently been modernised but upper-floor bedrooms are

reached by a steep stone Gothic staircase in the courtyard.

San Fantin, Campiello Fenice, San Marco 1930/A (tel: 041 5231401). A quiet hotel, once headquarters for the Venetians' rebellion against Austrian rule in 1848. Its façade is decorated with guns and cannon-balls.

Inexpensive Hotels
The choice of pleasant accommodation for visitors on a low budget is limited, but there are some gems of *pensioni* with historical or literary associations or fine views to compensate for any lack of luxury.

Bucintoro, Riva San Biagio, Castello 2135/A (tel: 041 5223240). The best view of Venice from any hotel is from here. All the bedroom windows overlook the Riva degli Schiavoni, the Basin of San Marco and the island of San Giorgio, the Salute and the Doges' Palace beyond. Run by a delightful family, it is cosy rather than smart and has its own restaurant, so offering half-board. A century ago it was lodgings for art students, particularly Americans, including James McNeill Whistler who relished the panorama and etched from its windows. Closed mid-November to March 1.

Calcina (tel: 041 5206466). Another fine view of water – in this case the Canale Giudecca – is from the Calcina, the small hotel on the Zattere, where Ruskin stayed while writing *The Stones of Venice.* Partly modernised and lacking some of its former modest charm, it is a friendly little hotel and a favourite with British visitors. Closed from December to January.

Fiorita, Campiello Nuovo, San Marco 3457/A (tel: 041 5234754). Among the most simple *pensioni*, the Fiorita is well-sited near the centre, welcoming, clean and uncomplicated; the comfortable rooms have no en suite baths, showers or lavatories but the public ones – which are always kept spotless – are just down the passage.

San Stafano, Campo Francesco Morosini, San Marco 2957 (tel: 041 5200166). This should not be confused with the similarly named but quite different Casa de' Stefani. It is a small, recently smartened-up hotel, which is situated on the San Marco side of the Accademia bridge.

Lido Hotels
Two gigantic relics of the heyday of the Lido are hotels designed for rich pre-1914 families. Both come alive during the Venice Film Festival which is concentrated on the Lido, and both are as expensive as one would expect from their glamorous associations.

Des Bains, Lungomare Marconi 17 (tel: 041 5265921). The doom-laden film *Death in Venice* was made here and the hotel exudes a suitably stately gloom. 258 rooms.

Excelsior, Lungomare Marconi 41 (tel: 041 5260201). This is a turn-of-the-century, mock-Moorish architectural fantasy with 230 rooms, half of them overlooking the sea.

Among the tall trees just inland from the famous beach stands the **Quattro Fontane**, Via 4 Fontane 16 (tel: 041 5260227), a comfortable, rambling house in an oddly alpine style with a modern wing. In summer, meals and drinks are served in the large garden, and a *vaporetto* stops near by at the Casino pier from lunchtime until 04.00 hours every half hour and takes passengers direct to San Marco.

CULTURE, ENTERTAINMENT, NIGHTLIFE

Venice enjoys a rich cultural life throughout the year. Apart from the Teatro la Fenice (Fenice Theatre), which presents opera in winter and concerts and recitals all year (currently in a marquee, after the original house was destroyed by fire), there are three other main theatres: L'Avogaria, Goldoni and Ridotto. Recitals are sometimes held in churches, notably the Pietà, the Ospedaletto, the Frari and San Stae. There are several cinemas, though films are always shown in Italian. Throughout the year special exhibitions are presented in the principal museums, at the Doges' Palace, on the island of San Giorgio and at the Palazzo Grassi. Often they are advertised with enormous banners in dull Venetian red inscribed in gold and hanging from the bridges over the Grand Canal.

Summer is the season of festivals. The **Biennale** modern art exhibition takes place every other year through the summer, focused on the 40 permanent pavilions in the **Giardini Publici** and galleries around town. The **Festival of Dance** is held in July and the **International Film Festival** is held on the Lido in late August/ early September.

Venice goes to bed – or at least home – early and not long after 22.00 hours, the alleys are quiet. A few bars remain open – notably **A Teatro**, Campo San Fantin, San Marco 1916 (tel: 041 5221052), which also serves food and sells newspapers and cigarettes; **Haig's Bar**, Campo del Giglio, San Marco 2477 (tel: 5289456), which is near the Gritti Palace Hotel; and **Il Caffè**, Campo Santa Margherita 2963, Dorsoduro (tel: 041 5287998) – as do those in the grander hotels.

Otherwise most nightlife is to be seen at the casinos, both of

It's easy to see why Napoleon called Piazza S Marco the most elegant drawing room in Europe

which have their own night-clubs. On the Canal Grande, the **Casino Municipale** is in the Palazzo Vendramin Calergi, Strada Nuova, Cannaregio 2040 (tel: 041 5297111) and is open from 15.00 to 03.00 hours from mid-September to mid-June; the rest of the year the **Casino Municipale**, Lungomare, G Marconi 4, Lido (tel: 041 5297111) is open on the Lido during the same hours, throughout which it is served by a half-hourly *vaporetto* direct from San Marco after 14.00 hours.

HOW TO BE A LOCAL

The best advice is: 'Don't try.' Venetians have always welcomed, or at least accepted, visitors, but only when these have come to live there and can speak Italian can they hope to be considered as 'a local', albeit a foreign one. However, it is fun to share the locals' daily routines of city life and this can easily be done. Take to crossing the Canal Grande by *traghetto* and stand up – as they do – during the brief voyage, even if the

gondola rocks in the wake of a *vaporetto.*

Shop in the Rialto markets, the Campo Santa Margherita, or buy fruit and vegetables from the barge moored by the Campo San Barnaba. Try drinking wine in one of the tiny wine-shops in the back alleys, or coffee in the hole-in-the-wall cafés without tables and chairs. Look out for modest *trattorie,* which are crowded with voluble Venetians at lunchtime.

Venetians themselves are formal in their dress – except at carnival-time – and expect visitors to look neat, if not formal, in their city. Beach clothes always look wrong in the city (although not, of

Venture off the beaten track and pick up a more unusual souvenir in one of Venice's old-fashioned wine shops

course, on the Lido) and are forbidden in most churches. Jackets and ties are expected in the grander hotels and restaurants, although informal clothes are allowed if presentable. It should be noted that formality is expected at the opera or theatre.

In summer, when it is usually hot, there is much more informality and open-necked shirts are usual wear. In spring and autumn, take light clothes but something warm to wear over them in the evening when

If you want to eat where the locals do, look out for the popular waterside trattorie

it may be cool. It can rain – occasionally for days on end – particularly in the spring, so be prepared. In winter it can be very cold indeed, and it can snow, so warm clothes and gloves are essential. The catastrophic high tide, the *acqua alta*, which can flood the city is most likely in late autumn but can occur at other seasons. Duckboard walkways are laid across the Piazza San Marco and other thoroughfares but do not extend throughout the city, so suitable footwear is essential. These improvised walkways are often narrow and unstable, so Venetians show more restraint in using them than anyone struggling for a place on a *vaporetto* might expect: patiently waiting their turn to cross. Some visitors in November and December take rubber waterboots with them, or buy them on arrival;

or simple plastic bags which cover the shoes and tie below the knee can be bought cheaply.

During the February *Carnevale*, those who want to wear fancy dress can buy, or even hire, it in the city if they do not bring it with them. The most elaborate costumes and masks are available in the many specialist shops but they are accordingly expensive. The most simple and effective fancy dress is simply a black cloak, a tricorn hat and a traditional white mask.

Pigeons might be a favourite with the visitors, but conservationists worry that they may be causing stone erosion

PERSONAL PRIORITIES

Venice is a safe city for women and children. Street crime is rare although burglary is a problem and pickpockets can be expected in crowds at the railway station during the holiday season. Unlike in some Italian cities, women walking alone at night are seldom pestered, particularly if they maintain a purposeful pace; if they are it is more likely to be by young male visitors to the city than by native Venetians. Hygienic necessities for women, and baby food and nappies are available in supermarkets and pharmacies as elsewhere in Europe.

CHILDREN

Children are unlikely to be as interested in art and architecture as their elders but there is much in Venice to fascinate them. For a start there is the constant jumping on and off boats, both *vaporetti* and *traghetto* gondolas, and looking out from the tops of the *campanili* of San Marco and San Giorgio. Watching the glass-blowers at work, even at one of the demonstration furnaces in the city, is enthralling and they need no persuading to start collecting little – and cheap – glass animals. Children usually enjoy Italian food, particularly pasta and ice cream, and their presence can enhance a meal, as Italian waiters usually love the under-eights.

Venice is a safe city for children and they can be sent off safely – but preferably not singly – to feed the pigeons in the Piazza San Marco or watch the water-borne traffic go by on the Grand Canal. Some families may prefer to stay on the Lido, where bicycles can be hired and the traffic is sparse, and there are fine sands and sea for swimming. There is a rather dusty playground in the **Giardini Publici** at the far eastern end of the Riva (*Vaporetto pier*: Giardini).

Older children may well enjoy the Museo Navale (► 52), with its beautifully constructed model ships, and the dungeons of the Palazzo Ducale (► 21), with its spine-tingling torture chambers.

TIGHT BUDGET

Venice need not be an expensive city. The Venetians' main mode of transport is free – walking; and a large plate of pasta with a glass of wine makes a satisfying and cheap meal. Varieties of rolls, brioches and biscuits with coffee can fill the gaps between meals quite economically.

For cheap accommodation enquire at the tourist information offices (*Ente Provinciale per il Turismo*) at Calle Ascensione 71C, Piazza San Marco (tel: 041 5298727), Santa Lucia railway station (tel: 041 5298727) or at the Piazzale Roma (tel: 041 5298727). There is a well-run youth hostel, **Ostello Venezia**, Fondamenta delle Zitelle, Giudecca 86 (tel: 041 5238211) on Giudecca Island. Send a written reservation, especially if you are planning to come in the summer. There are also a number of religious institutions that offer accommodation (sometimes in a dormitory) and two, **Foresteria Valdese** at Santa Maria Formosa (tel: 041 5286797), and **Istituto Suaore Canossiane**, Ponte Piccolo, Giudecca 428 (tel: 041 5222157, women only) are open all the year round. You will find others on a list produced annually by the local tourist organisation; copies are available at the San Marco office.

For recommended inexpensive hotels in the city, ► **Accommodation**, 85.

SPECIAL EVENTS

Winter
In winter the main event is *Carnevale*, which was abolished by the French in 1797 but revived in 1980 with great success. At first largely a Venetian festival, it is now international and, some complain, over-elaborate. For ten days before Lent, masks and fancy dress – which can be bought or hired in the city – are worn all day and most of the night. A daily programme of events includes dancing at night in a *campo*, where mulled wine and traditional sugared cakes are sold from stalls. Ask at the Italian State Tourist Office for the exact dates of the *Carnevale*.

Spring
On La Sensa, the Sunday after Ascension Day, the Mayor and Patriarch of Venice re-enact the ceremony of the **Marriage of Venice with the Sea**. In the old days, the Doge would be rowed out to sea in his ceremonial barge, the *Bucintoro*, to cast a gold wedding ring into the Adriatic, but the occasion is now only a faint echo of the original. The **Vogalonga** regatta – a 20-mile (32km) rowing race in which anyone can join in any type of oared boat – takes place on the first Sunday after Ascension Day. Boats leave at 09.30 hours from Sant'Elena, at the eastern end of the city.

Summer
Cultural events are the **Festival of Dance** in July, the **International Film Festival** on

Festivals and regattas have always been a colourful part of the Venetian calendar

the Lido in late August/early September and, every odd-numbered year, from June to September, the **Biennale** modern art exhibition. The **Festa del Redentore**, which involves the building of a bridge of boats across the Giudecca Canal to the church of the Redentore, and was

begun as a festival in thanksgiving for the ending of a plague more than four centuries ago, is held on the third weekend in July.

On the first Sunday in September, the **Regata Storica**, the most spectacular event of the Venetian year, is held. It involves gondola races and a procession up the Grand Canal of boats and barges manned by Venetians in historic costume.

Autumn

The opera season opens at the Palafenice in November. Important art exhibitions and a Festival of Contemporary Music are held.

On 21 November the **Festa della Madonna della Salute** – a procession across the Grand Canal on floating bridges to the church of the Salute to give thanks for the ending of another plague in the 17th century – takes place.

On a hot summer day, where better than the beach? However, many are private and charge a fee

SPORT

Other than the regattas for gondoliers and watermen, there is little sport in Venice itself, although there is a stadium on the Isola di Sant'Elena at the extreme eastern tip of the city. Sporting activity is largely confined to the Lido. There are the Tennis Club Venezia, Lungomare Marconi 41d (tel: 041 5260335) and the Tennis Club Caí del Moro, Via Ferruccio Parri 6 (tel: 041 770801), and the major hotels have their own courts. Also on the island is the Venice Riding Club (*Circolo Ippico Veneziano*), Ca' Bianca (tel: 041 5261820), and the Excelsior Hotel offers sailing in summer.

Swimming
The Lido is the bathing-place of Venice but much of its seven-mile (11km) beach is privately owned, and a hefty fee is payable on each stretch for changing facilities and deck chairs. The hire of beach huts is particularly expensive.
The only public swimming pool in Venice is that at the Hotel Cipriani and that is reserved for those staying, or buying pricey non-residents' tickets.
There are good bathing beaches on the mainland east of Venice between the landing-stage at Punta Sabbioni (Ferry No 14 from San Zaccaria or the Lido) and Lido di Jesolo, which is connected to Venice by a bus service from the Piazzale Roma.

Practical Matters

Above: *trains arrive at Santa Lucia station*
Right: *carnival mask*

101

BEFORE YOU GO

WHAT YOU NEED

● Required
○ Suggested
▲ Not required

	UK	Germany	USA	Netherlands	Spain
Passport	●	●	●	●	●
Visa	▲	▲	▲	▲	▲
Onward or return ticket	▲	▲	▲	▲	▲
Health inoculations	▲	▲	▲	▲	▲
Health documentation (➤ 123, Health)	●	●	●	●	●
Travel insurance	○	○	○	○	○
Driving licence (national with Italian translation or international)	●	●	●	●	●
Car insurance certificate (if own car)	●	●	●	●	●
Car registration document (if own car)	●	●	●	●	●

WHEN TO GO

Venice

High season

Low season

6°C	8°C	12°C	15°C	20°C	23°C	26°C	25°C	21°C	16°C	12°C	7°C
JAN	FEB	MAR	APR	MAY	JUN	JUL	AUG	SEP	OCT	NOV	DEC

 Wet   Cloud   Sun   Sunshine/Showers

TOURIST OFFICES

In the UK
Italian State Tourist Office (ENIT)
1 Princes Street
London W1R 8AY
☎ 020 7408 1254
Fax 020 7493 6695

In the US
Italian State Tourist Office (ENIT)
630 Fifth Avenue
Suite 1565
New York
☎ (212) 245 4822

NATIONAL POLICE (Polizia di Stato) 113

CITY POLICE (Carabinieri) 112

FIRE (Vigili del Fuoco) 115

AMBULANCE (Ambulància) 118

WHEN YOU ARE THERE

ARRIVING

There are direct flights from most major European cities but no direct intercontinental flights. Scheduled flights arrive at Venice's Marco Polo airport, while the city's second airport, Treviso, caters mostly for charter flights. Trains to Venice arrive at Venezia Santa Lucia station, located at the head of the Grand Canal.

Marco Polo Airport
Distance to city centre

13km

Journey times

🚆	50 minutes
🚌	25 minutes
🚗	15 minutes

Treviso Airport
Distance to city centre

30km

Journey times

🚆	N/A
🚌	45 minutes
🚗	35 minutes

MONEY

Italy's currency is the Italian lira (plural lire), abbreviated to Lit, L or £, and issued in coins of 5, 10, 20, 50, 100, 200 and 500 lire and notes of 1,000, 2,000, 5,000, 10,000, 50,000 and 100,000 lire. On 1 Jan 1999 the euro became the official currency of Italy and the Italian lira became a denomination of the euro. Lira notes and coins continue to be legal tender during a transitional period. Euro bank notes and coins are likely to be introduced by January 2002.

TIME

Venice is one hour ahead of Greenwich Mean Time (GMT + 1), but from late March, when clocks are put forward one hour, until late October, Italian summer time (GMT + 2) operates.

CUSTOMS

YES

Goods obtained Duty Free inside the EU or goods bought outside the EU (Limits):
Alcohol (over 22% vol): 1L or Alcohol (not over 22% vol): 2L *and*
Still table wine: 2L,
Cigarettes: 200 *or* Cigars: 50 *or* Tobacco: 250gm
Perfume: 60ml
Toilet water: 250ml
Goods bought Duty and Tax Paid for own use inside the EU (Guidance Levels):
Alcohol (over 22% vol): 10L
Alcohol (not over 22% vol): 20L *and* Wine (max 60L sparkling): 90L Beer: 110L
Cigarettes: 800, Cigars: 200, Tobacco: 1kg
Perfume and Toilet Water: no limit
You must be 17 or over to benefit from alcohol and tobacco allowances.

NO

Drugs, firearms, ammunition, offensive weapons, obscene material, unlicensed animals.

CONSULATES

USA in Milan 02 290351	**UK** 041 5227207	**Germany** 041 5237675	**Netherlands** 041 5283416	**Spain** 041 5203709

WHEN YOU ARE THERE

TOURIST OFFICES

Head Office
● Palazetto del Selva
  Giardinetti Reale
  San Marco
  ☎ 041 5226356

Branches

**International Arrivals Hall
(airport office)**
● Marco Polo airport
  ☎ 041 5415887

**Ferrovia Santa Lucia (train
station office)**
  ☎ 041 5298727

● Piazza San Marco 71
  ☎ 041 5298727

● Gran Viale Santa Maria
  Elisabetta 6 (Lido office)
  ☎ 041 5265721

NATIONAL HOLIDAYS

J	F	M	A	M	J	J	A	S	O	N	D
2		(1)	(2)	1			1			1	3

1 Jan	New Year's Day
6 Jan	Epiphany
Mar/Apr	Easter Monday
25 Apr	Liberation Day and patron saint's day (San Marco)
1 May	Labour Day
15 Aug	Assumption of the Virgin
1 Nov	All Saints' Day
8 Dec	Feast of the Immaculate Conception
25 Dec	Christmas Day
26 Dec	Santo Stefano

OPENING HOURS

○ Shops   ● Attractions/museums
● Offices   ○ Churches
● Banks   ○ Pharmacies

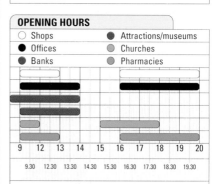

9	12	13	14	15	16	17	18	19	20
9.30	12.30	13.30	14.30	15.30	16.30	17.30	18.30	19.30	

Some tourist shops and supermarkets may also open
outside the times shown above, especially in summer.
Most food shops close on Wednesday afternoons,
while many other shops close Monday mornings
(except in summer), and may close Saturday
afternoon. Most shops are closed on Sundays.

Some churches are permanently closed except
during services; state-run museums usually close
Mondays, and some museums, such as the Correr,
Palazzo Ducale and Guggenheim, stay open all day.

DRIVE ON THE
RIGHT

TOILETS
FREE

PUBLIC TRANSPORT

Vaporetto The *vaporetto*, or waterbus, is operated by the public transport system, ACTV. The main routes run every 10 to 20 minutes during the day. Services are reduced in the evening, especially after midnight. Fast *diretto* boats are more expensive than those that stop at every landing stage. You can buy a ticket for each journey at a ticket office on the pier (if there is one), or pay more for a ticket on board, but If you intend to make six or more journeys in a day, buy a 24-hour ticket (*biglietto turistico*). If you plan 10 or more journeys within three days buy a 72-hour ticket; or buy a *blochetta* of 10 or more tickets to be used over any period. All tickets must be date-stamped by the automatic machine on the pier before boarding. If you are staying a week, you can buy a weekly *abbonamento* from ticket offices.

Gondola A gondola is undoubtedly the most enjoyable means of transport in the city, but also the most expensive. Fares are governed by a tariff and should be about 80,000 lire for a 50-minute trip, with a surcharge for night trips after 20.00 hours, but, as gondoliers are notorious for overcharging, it is often easiest to establish terms by ordering a gondola via your tour representative or hotel staff. For a memorable outing, take a two-hour gondola ride down the Grand Canal with a picnic supper on board. Alternatively, consider a cruise operated during the summer months by flotillas of gondolas packed with tourists and entertained by singers – providing an ideal opportunity to explore the waterways at an affordable price.

Traghetto Ferry gondolas – *traghetti* – cross the Grand Canal between special piers at seven different points, providing a vital service for pedestrians. They are indicated by yellow street sign, illustrated with a tiny gondola symbol. The very reasonable fare is paid to the gondolier on embarkation.

CAR RENTAL

The leading international car rental companies have offices at Marco Polo airport. Book a car in advance (essential in peak season) either direct or through a travel agent. Bear in mind that driving in the centre of Venice itself is not possible.

TAXIS

Water-taxis can be hired from 16 water-taxi ranks, including ones at the airport, the railway station, Piazzale Roma, San Marco and the Lido. They can also be ordered by telephone (tel: 041 5229750). Fares are regulated by a tariff.

DRIVING

Speed limit on motorways (*autostrade*): **130kph**

Speed limit on main roads: **110kph**
Speed limit on secondary roads: **90kph**

Speed limit in towns: **50kph**

Seat belts must be worn in front seats at all times and in rear seats where fitted.

Random breath-testing is frequent in Italy. Limit: 80μg per 100ml of blood.

Fuel (*benzina*) is more expensive than in the US and most European countries. Filling stations all sell unleaded petrol (*senza piombo*), but do not always accept credit cards. They are generally open Monday to Saturday 07.00–12.30 and 15.00–19.30 hours. Motorway service stations open 24 hours.

In the event of a breakdown ring the Automobile Club d'Italia on 116, giving your location, registration number and type of car, and the nearest ACI office will tow you to the nearest ACI garage. This service is free to foreign vehicles, but you will need to produce your car documentation and passport.

CENTIMETRES

INCHES

PERSONAL SAFETY

To help prevent crime:
• Do not carry more cash around with you than you need
• Beware of pickpockets in markets, tourist sights or crowded places

The main police station, at Via San Nicoladi 22, Marghera (☎ 041 2715511) has a special department to deal with visitors' problems

Police assistance:
☎ **112 or 113**

TELEPHONES

Public telephones take 100, 200 and 500 lire coins, or tokens (*gettone*) valued at 200 lire, or phonecards (*schede telfoniche*) which can be bought from SIP offices (the state telephone company) or tabacchi, bars and news stands, for 5,000, 10,000 or 15,000 lire. You have to break off the marked corner of the phonecard before use.

International Dialling Codes

from Venice to:

UK:	00 44
Germany:	00 49
USA:	00 1
Netherlands:	00 31
Spain	00 34

POST

Most post offices open Monday to Friday from 08.00 to 14.00 hours. Some also open on Saturday morning. The main post office (*ufficio postale*) at Palazzo delle Poste (near the Rialto Bridge), is open Monday to Friday 08.15–17.30 hours, and Saturday 08.15– 13.00 hours. You can also buy stamps (*francobolli*) at tobacconists.

ELECTRICITY

The power supply is 220 volts, but is suitable for 240-volt appliances.

Sockets accept two-round-pin Continental-style plugs.
US visitors should bring a voltage transformer.

TIPS/GRATUITIES

Yes ✓ No ✗		
Restaurants (if service not included)	✓	10–15%
Cafés/bars (if service not included)	✓	change
Tour guides	✓	L1,000
Hairdressers	✓	change
Water-taxis	✓	10%
Chambermaids	✓	L3,000
Porters	✗	L2,000
Theatre/cinema usherettes	✓	change
Cloakroom attendants	✓	change
Toilets	✓	L100 +

PHOTOGRAPHY

What to photograph: the Grand Canal, St Mark's Square, Doge's Palace, hidden alleys and waterways, reflections on the canals and the colourful houses on Burano.

Best time to photograph: early morning or late evening, when the light is at its best.

Where to buy film: film and camera batteries are readily available from specialist shops and some tourist shops.

HEALTH

Insurance

Nationals of EU and certain other countries can get medical treatment in Italy with the relevant documentation (Form E111 for Britons), although private medical insurance is still advised and is essential for all other visitors.

Dental Services

Dental treatment is expensive in Italy, but should be covered by private medical insurance. A list of *dentisti* can be found in the yellow pages of the telephone directory.

Sun Advice

The sunniest (and hottest) months are June, July and August. You are advised to use a strong sunblock and avoid the midday sun.

Drugs

Prescription and non-prescription drugs and medicines are available from a pharmacy (*farmacia*), distinguished by a green cross.

Safe Water

Tap water is generally safe to drink unless marked *acqua non potabile*. Drink plenty of water in hot weather.

CONCESSIONS

Students

Holders of an International Student Identity Card may be able to obtain some concessions on travel, entrance fees, and so on. A 'Rolling Venice' card for those aged 14–30, available from tourist offices, offers discounts in certain hotels, theatres, shops and restaurants as well as a booklet with useful budget information for the young. The main youth hostel in Venice is Ostello Venezia, Fondamenta della Zitelle, on Giudecca (tel: 041 5238211). Book well in advance for the summer.

Senior Citizens

Venice is a popular destination for older travellers although, due to the limited transport system, you must be prepared for lots of walking. The best deals are available through tour operators who specialise in holidays for senior citizens.

CLOTHING SIZES

USA	UK	Europe		
36	36	46		Suits
38	38	48		
40	40	50		
42	42	52		
44	44	54		
46	46	56		
8	7	41		Shoes
8.5	7.5	42		
9.5	8.5	43		
10.5	9.5	44		
11.5	10.5	45		
12	11	46		
14.5	14.5	37		Shirts
15	15	38		
15.5	15.5	39/40		
16	16	41		
16.5	16.5	42		
17	17	43		
6	8	34		Dresses
8	10	36		
10	12	38		
12	14	40		
14	16	42		
16	18	44		
6	4.5	38		Shoes
6.5	5	38		
7	5.5	39		
7.5	6	39		
8	6.5	40		
8.5	7	41		

WHEN DEPARTING

- Contact the airport on the day before leaving to ensure the flight details are unchanged.
- The airport departure tax, payable when you leave Italy, is already included in the cost of the airline ticket.

LANGUAGE

Many Venetians speak some English but they really appreciate it when foreigners make an effort to speak Italian, however badly. It is relatively straightforward to have a go at some basics, as the words are pronounced as they are spelt. Every vowel and consonant (except 'h') is sounded and, as a general rule, the stress falls on the penultimate syllable. Here is a basic vocabulary to help with the most essential words and expressions.

hotel	*albergo*	rate	*tariffa*
room	*camera*	breakfast	*prima colazione*
single/double	*singola/doppia*	toilet	*toilette*
for one/two	*per una/due*	bath	*bagno*
nights	*notta/i*	shower	*doccia*
for one/two	*per una/due*	key	*chiave*
people	*persona/e*	room service	*servizio da*
reservation	*prenotazione*		*camera*

bank	*banco*	one	*uno, una*
exchange office	*cambio*	two	*due*
post office	*posta*	three	*tre*
foreign	*cambio con*	four	*quattro*
exchange	*l'estero*	five	*cinque*
pound sterling	*sterlina*	six	*sei*
American dollar	*dollaro*	seven	*sette*
coin	*moneta*	eight	*otto*
banknote	*banconota*	nine	*nove*
traveller's	*assegno*	ten	*dieci*
cheque	*turistico*	hundred	*cento*
credit card	*carta di credito*	thousand	*mille*
exchange rate	*tasso di cambio*	hundred thousand	*centomila*
commmission	*commissione*	million	*milione*

restaurant	*ristorante*	chicken	*pollo*
café	*caffè*	beef	*manzo*
table	*tavolo*	veal	*vitello*
menu	*menù/carta*	lamb	*agnello*
set menu	*menù turístico*	egg	*uovo*
wine list	*lista dei vini*	stuffed	*farcito*
lunch	*pranzo/*	baked	*al forno*
	colazione	bread	*pane*
dinner	*cena*	beans	*fagioli*
starter	*il primo*	mushrooms	*funghi*
main course	*il secondo*	rice	*riso*
dish of the day	*piatto del*	chips	*patate fritte*
	giorno	garlic	*aglio*
waiter/waitress	*cameriere/a*	cheese	*formaggio*
the bill	*il conto*	dessert	*dolci*
all together	*tutto insieme*	ice-cream	*gelato*

aeroplane	*aeroplano*	seat	*posto*
airport	*aeroporto*	non-smoking	*vietato fumare*
train	*treno*	reserved	*prenotato/*
train station	*stazione*		*riservato*
	ferroviaria	where is…?	*dov'è*
bus	*autobus*	left	*sinistra*
bus station	*autostazione*	right	*destra*
ferry	*traghetto*	straight ahead	*dritto*
ticket	*biglietto*	does this boat	*questo*
single/return	*andata solo/*	go to…?	*traghetto va*
	andata e		*a…?*
	ritorno	the next stop	*la prossima*
first/second	*prima/seconda*		*fermata*
class	*classe*	where are we?	*dove siamo?*
ticket office	*biglietteria*	direct	*diretto*
timetable	*orario*	passport	*passoporto*

yes	*sì*	how much?	*quanto?*
no	*no*	when?	*quando?*
please	*per favore*	what?	*cosa?*
thank you	*grazie*	where?	*dove?*
hello	*ciao*	here	*qui*
goodbye	*arriverderci*	large	*grande*
goodnight	*buona notte*	small	*piccolo*
sorry	*mi dispacie*	hot	*caldo*
OK, don't	*prego*	cold	*freddo*
mention it		good	*buono*
help!	*aiuto!*	expensive	*caro*
open	*aperto*	cheap	*a buon mercato*
closed	*chiuso*	many/much	*molto*
today	*oggi*	entrance	*entrata*
tomorrow	*domani*	exit	*uscita*
yesterday	*ieri*	all	*tutto*
hour	*ora*	inside	*dentro*
day	*giorno*	come in!	*avanti!*
week	*settimana*	I do not	*non la capisco*
year	*anno*	understand	

A VENETIAN GLOSSARY

acqua alta	a high tide that floods Venice	*fondamenta*	waterside promenade
basilica	cathedral	*molo*	quay
calle	pedestrian alley	*palazzo*	palace
campanile	bell-tower	*piano nobile*	principal floor
campo	small square	*rio terra*	filled-in canal, now a wide calle
casa, ca'	square	*riva*	wide waterside promenade
cortile	a large house or palazzo	*salone*	principal reception room of palazzo

109

INDEX

Acknowledgements

The Automobile Association would like to thank the following photographers and libraries for their assistance in the preparation of this book:

GALLERIA DELL ACCADEMIA 47

MARY EVANS PICTURE LIBRARY 10b, 11, 12b, 12c

NATURE PHOTOGRAPHERS LTD 62 (N A Callow), 66 (P R Sterry), 67 (R Tidman), 68 (P R Sterry), 69 (R Tidman), 70 (R Bush), 72 (P R Sterry)

SPECTRUM COLOUR LIBRARY Front Cover (c) (Gondolier and Rialto Bridge), 25, 48, 56/57, 59, 60/61, 64, 100

THE STOCK MARKET 16/17, 22/23, 98/99

The remaining photographs are held in the Association's own library (AA PHOTOLIBRARY) and were taken by Richard Newton with the exception of:

Front Cover (d), 1, 4b, 5b, 8b, 36/37 which were taken by Dario Miterdiri; Front Cover (a), (b), Back Cover, 2, 4a, 4c, 5a, 6a, 6b, 7a, 7b, 8a, 9a, 9b, 9c, 10a, 12a, 26/27, 52, 75, 94, 101a, 101b, 106b which were taken by Clive Sawyer; 106a was taken by Barrie Smith, 106c was taken by Antony Souter

Contributors
This edition revised by Teresa Fisher. Additional text by Teresa Fisher.